SIGNS OF THE SAVIOUR'S RETURN

SIGNS

OF

THE SAVIOUR'S RETURN

by

THEODORE C. DANSON SMITH
B.Th., F.M.E., Th.D.

Author of 'From the Rainbow to the Rapture'

Published by

B. McCALL BARBOUR
28 George IV Bridge,
Edinburgh, Scotland

First Printed   May 1979
Reprinted   May 1981
Reprinted   May 1987

ISBN 0 7132 0028 6

Printed in Great Britain
at the University Printing House, Oxford

AUTHOR'S PREFACE

In presenting this book with its great message of certainty for the Christian and challenge to those who know not Christ, I would like to acknowledge with gratitude the tremendous influence of my parents and especially my father, whose poems I quote frequently herein. It was they who taught me the way of salvation and encouraged me to study Bible prophecy, and since my early teens this subject has enthralled me.

I would also express my appreciation to The Zondervan Corporation, The Bethany Fellowship, The Sword of the Lord Publishers, and various other copyright holders for permitting me to quote some of their material.

CONTENTS

INTRODUCTION

Signs of the near return of the Lord Jesus Christ abound today on every hand. We live in times that are difficult, yet they are times which are thrilling and exciting! For the true Christian, the realisation that our Saviour's return for His Own is at hand makes the prospect glorious and exhilarating. On the other hand, the outlook for those who have not been redeemed by the precious blood of Christ is gloomy and foreboding. They face the Great Tribulation and finally a lost eternity.

The signs of the times are apparent. We live in the last days—if not the last moments—of the Age of Grace. This period of time has lasted for nearly two thousand years. It has been the dispensation during which the Church has been formed and built up. It will finish when the trumpet sounds and all born-again believers are caught up to meet the Lord in the air. Oh that people would repent of their sins and accept Christ as their Saviour NOW —while they have the opportunity!

The signs of the Saviour's return constantly multiply. In the pages that follow we shall consider certain signs which deal with certain aspects of the Lord's return. There are many other signs which space prevents us from considering.

Chapter I

THE JEWISH SIGN

One of the greatest signs that the Saviour's return is near is the Jew!

A. The Scattering of Israel

After the Jewish nation's dispersal in A.D. 70 when Titus the Roman commander captured Jerusalem after a siege of one hundred and forty-three days there was nothing worthwhile to report about the people until 1948 when Israel became a nation again.   The land had been fought over frequently during the many centuries which passed. Moslems, Crusaders, Turks and others were involved. Dr. Wilbur M. Smith comments: "On April 24, 1920, the mandate for Palestine and Transjordan was assigned to Great Britain, and for nearly 30 years she suffered one reverse after another in her attempt to rule this country. On May 14, 1948, the British mandate terminated and the National Council at Tel Aviv proclaimed the State of Israel."

Today, the Jew is a sign!   Israel is a daily word in our homes.   The press and the broadcasters refer to this nation continually.   Israel is at the centre of the earth— physically as well as politically.   God has restored His earthly people to part of their land, for eventually it will spread out much further than its present boundaries. Israel is a nation to be reckoned with, and a nation to be respected.

Dr. M. R. DeHaan says: "First and foremost among the signs of the Lord's return is the miraculous restoration of the Israelite nation in the ancient land of Palestine after twenty-five hundred years of dispersion among the nations without a national existence. . . . The Israelites have been hated and persecuted, maligned and oppressed. Attempts at their complete extermination were tried over and over again, from the days of Haman to the present time. In spite of all these efforts, they have never perished. They were not lost among the nations, but retained their identity as a people, imperishable and eternal as the promises of God."

The Scattering of Israel is Biblical. It was foretold in Scripture in chapters such as Leviticus 26 and Deuteronomy 28, 29 and 30. But, *the restoration of Israel* is also foretold in the Word of God. The Bible states that they will be regathered to their land just before their Messiah comes—the Lord Jesus Christ. In Isaiah chapter 11, in Jeremiah chapter 33, in Ezekiel chapter 36 and in Amos chapter 9, as well as in other passages, the Bible states emphatically that Israel will be re-established and this is a tremendous sign of the near return of Christ.

Years ago, Rev. E. L. Langston wrote: "God in His Word has predicted that in the last days certain things must happen to Palestine, to the Jews, and to Jerusalem. Are not these things now coming to pass? Is it not significant that, during the last war, the edict went forth that Great Britain was prepared to give facilities for the Jews to be restored to their own land? . . . According to the prophetic Scriptures, the Messiah cannot come unless the Jews are restored to their land, and are dwelling in that land. When He comes, Zechariah tells us (ch. 12:10 R.V.)—'They shall look unto Me Whom they have pierced' and mourn for their sins. After a period of mourning and affliction this race will be transformed, become all-righteous, and fulfil the great function for which God has preserved them throughout all the past ages."

B. THE SALVATION OF ISRAEL

Today many in Israel are looking for their Messiah to come. Their religious leaders say that prophecy teaches that the nation will prosper, the Temple will be rebuilt and then Messiah will come to reign. The Bible says that this is so—although the false Christ—the Man of Sin—will come first and deceive them. The Lord, however, will save His ancient people. They will experience His salvation.

It is manifest today that the Lord is on the side of the Jews. In each conflict with the Arabs since 1948 they have been victorious—despite being heavily outnumbered by armies with vast amounts of modern equipment. In 1967 there was the Six-Day War and Israel was victorious. Various reports tell how the Israelis captured several Arab generals. When they were questioned, they said they knew that the Israelis had a good Air Force, but they did not know of their large cavalry division. They were told by their captors that they had no cavalry! The Arab generals replied that they had seen them—an army of men on horseback dressed in white uniforms—and they had killed thousands of Arab soldiers. Surely, this was a case of God's Cavalry in action. Elisha and his servant saw them long ago at Samaria (2 Kings 6:17). Today, the Jew is back in the land—to stay!

The so-called "problem" regarding the Arab-Israeli dispute will continue until the Antichrist makes his treaty with Israel during the Great Tribulation—a treaty which he will eventually break. The nation Israel will then suffer terribly and Christ will thereafter come back in power and great glory to Jerusalem to rule as King of kings and Lord of lords.

God's dealings with His earthly people resume, in proper, AFTER the Rapture of the Church. Dr. J. Dwight Pentecost has stated: "God today is calling out from among both Jew and Gentile a people for His name (Acts 15:14). God will not move toward the fulfilment of these prophecies for Israel until the Church, which is His present age program, has been removed by translation. What is to be concluded is that God is getting the stage set for this great drama, is getting the actors all in place, so that at a moment's notice He could move to fulfil these momentous events following the anticipated rapture of the Church. Coming events are casting their shadows before them. . . . Beloved of God, when we can see the foreshadowing of these very things on the horizon, so that the Federated States of Europe at any time could announce its support for Israel in the Arab-Israeli dispute in order to prevent Russian encroachment, how near must the coming of the Lord for His Own be?"

Yes, indeed, the Jewish sign is an important one! Christ is coming to reign for a thousand years on the throne of David at Jerusalem. But, first, He must come for His Bride—the Church, which consists of every born-again soul since the Day of Pentecost when the Church was born. The Bible says "The night is far spent, the day is at hand" (Romans 13:12). It also says "The coming of the Lord draweth nigh" (James 5:8).

Dr. Charles G. Trumbull, writing of the Jewish sign, says: "Christ is the theme of the Bible. Prophecy, centering about Christ, is the dominant note of the Bible. The Second Coming of Christ—being His personal, visible, bodily return to establish His Kingdom on earth and to reign over Israel and the world for a thousand years, after which will come 'a new heaven and a new earth' (Revelation 21:1)—is the goal, climax and consummation of Bible prophecy. As we study God's greatest sign, the Jew, let us remember that Israel never can fulfil God's destiny for her until Christ comes again. His coming is near."

Israel as a nation is yet to be the most important nation on earth—far ahead of the United States, or Great Britain, or Russia. The day is coming when she will repent as a people and acclaim the Lord Jesus Christ as her Messiah and King. The apostle Paul wrote in Romans 10:1—"Brethren, my heart's desire and prayer to God for Israel is, that they might be saved". Israel will experience God's salvation, for Paul says in Romans 11 verses 25 and 26: "Blindness in part is happened to Israel, until the fulness of the Gentiles be come in. And so all Israel shall be saved." Israel for centuries has been blind spiritually, but the day is at hand when her eyes will be opened and she will see. "The fulness of the Gentiles" is a phrase which refers to the close of the Age of Grace. The period known as "the fulness of the Gentiles" started at Pentecost and will cease with the Rapture of the Church.

Dr. John F. Walvoord, who is not only a great scholar but is also an authority on prophecy, states: "The deliverance of 'all Israel' is not a process but an event. The time of the event is clearly when the Deliverer comes out of Zion, an event following the return of Christ in His second coming. The prophesied deliverance is, therefore, a future event and a single event. . . . The future revelation of Christ to Israel will fulfil these predictions and bring the prophesied time of blessing for God's ancient people. . . . The restoration of Israel as a nation involves the Davidic covenant. It involves Israel's continuance as a nation and possession of the land. It involves the separation of the purposes of God for the church, believers in this age, and for Israel."

Yes, Israel as a nation is yet to experience God's salvation. Today, some Jews are being saved—as they repent of their sins and put their trust in Christ as their personal Saviour. The nation, however, is being re-gathered.

C. THE SYMBOLS OF ISRAEL

Three different plants are used in Scripture as Symbols of Israel. These are *the Vine, the Fig Tree* and *the Olive Tree*.

It is interesting to note that *the Vine* is symbolic of Israel in Old Testament times. In Psalm 80 verses 8-11 we are told of the Vine brought out of Egypt and planted in the Holy Land. Then, we see how it grew and stretched from the Mediterranean Sea eastward. The Vine had ample room for growth and God's hand was on it for blessing, but all it yielded was "wild grapes"! (Isaiah 5:1,

2). It was useless! Israel, as a nation, in Old Testament times, was useless and fruitless. It was cast off and burned up.

The Fig Tree is a symbol of Israel in the present age. The Lord Jesus Christ gave the symbol of the Fig Tree as a sign of His near return, when He said in Matthew 24:32 and 33: "Now learn a parable of the fig tree; When his branch is yet tender and putteth forth leaves, ye know that summer is nigh: So likewise ye, when ye shall see all these things, know that He is near, even at the doors".

Again quoting Dr. Trumbull, he says: "The return of the Lord and King is the great hope both of the Church and of Israel. The divinely ordained destiny of each awaits Christ's Coming. The glorious goal of neither one can be attained until Christ comes again. But this is a sure, unfailing hope, and the signs of its near fulfilment are multiplying before our eyes. The fig tree is a Scriptural symbol or type of the Jew. . . . Is the fig tree beginning to put forth leaves? Is there any reason to believe that the fig tree is now budding? Yes, there are impressive evidences of this—indeed, overwhelmingly convincing signs. There has been a putting forth of leaves in our generation that has not occurred before in the nineteen centuries since our Lord spoke those words."

In 1917 when General Allenby captured Jerusalem without firing a shot there were hardly any Jews in the land. Today, there are several million! The land is prospering in a most remarkable way. The desert is blossoming in fulfilment of Scripture. Roses are growing in what was the desert a short while ago. Vast crops are being grown. The mineral wealth of the nation is tremendous. This surely is a sign that the coming of the Lord Jesus Christ for His Own is at hand!

The other symbol is that of *the Olive Tree.* This is one of the most fruitful and useful of all trees. Olive oil was used in Bible times for lighting the home and for the healing of wounds. It was used for the anointing of kings and prophets. It has refreshing as well as healing properties.

The wood of the Olive Tree was used for making furniture for the Temple as well as for houses. The Olive Tree also lives to a great age—reputed to be about a thousand years—and it brings forth fruit in old age! The Jew has been useless to God in the past, but his day of blessing and usefulness as a nation is just ahead. The Lord God will soon take up and use His ancient earthly people.

> "The Fig Tree now is budding,
> And Israel takes her place,
> Acclaimed now as a nation,
> Not just a scattered race.
>
> The 'Gentile Times' are ending,
> Full many signs this say;
> The shout—the archangel's summons—
> Perhaps may sound today!"
>
> J. Danson Smith.

D. THE SOVEREIGN OF ISRAEL

The Sovereign of Israel will be none other than her rejected King of long ago—the Lord Jesus Christ! The Bible makes it clear that this ancient people who once cried "Away with Him! Crucify Him!" will crown Him King. He will be their Sovereign!

The Scriptures are being read and studied today in the land of Israel as never before. In schools, colleges and synagogues the Old Testament is read and believed. Some of the Jewish politicians openly base their decisions on the Old Testament and upon God's promises. The New Testament, too, is being ready by many, and the once despised and rejected Christ of Calvary is seen as a great religious leader.

Dr. Oswald J. Smith of Toronto says: "Now a complete change has taken place. His name is more or less freely used both in conversation and in books. Great Jewish scholars, not only in the United States and Europe, but also in Palestine, have written about Him at length and even produced sketches of His life, so that today He is rapidly being recognized as a great religious teacher by leading Jews the world over.   Such a change is phenomenal indeed to those who knew Jewry and the bitter hatred towards the Nazarene.   It is evident that God is preparing the hearts of the Jewish people for the reception of Jesus Christ as their Messiah, and that the time draws near when He is to come again.''

Hearts are being prepared for the coming of Christ *as King*.

The Bible tells us that the Throne of David shall never be destroyed (Luke 1:31-33).   The Lord Jesus Christ is to reign as Israel's Sovereign for ever.   The promise was first given to David in 2 Samuel 7 verses 4 to 17.   The Jewish nation is yet to be the greatest—for her King—the Lord Jesus Christ—will be ''King of kings and Lord of lords'', as John says in Revelation 19 verse 16.   Here, He is seen as leading the armies of heaven to destroy the Antichrist and the armies of the nations at Armageddon.   This will take place approximately seven years after He comes for His Own blood-bought Bride.

George D. Beckwith, in his book *God's Prophetic Plan* writes: ''In the Kingdom Age the Jews will possess their land.   They will build the temple, and sacrifices will be offered again.   The government will be set up.   The 'Sheep nations' of the earth will be blessed through Israel.   Many will say to the Jews, 'We will go with you; for we have heard that God is with you' (Zechariah 8:20-23).   Jesus will say to the 'Goat nations'—'Depart from Me, ye cursed, into everlasting fire' (Matthew 25:41).   Jesus will be King, and His Church will reign with Him.   He will rule on the throne of His father David.''

As Sovereign of Israel Christ will be supreme.   He will not only make the Jewish people a blessing, but He will bring peace to a warring world, and He will restore order out of chaos.   Dr. S. Franklin Logsdon has said: ''He must come back to the scene where the world at large thinks He was abjectly defeated.   He must come back to the place where He was rejected in order to be acclaimed.   He must come back to the realm which is now dominated by Satan in order to bind the 'strong man' who has deceived the nations. He must come back to the scene where man has so miserably failed in governmental policies and procedures in order to reign supreme! And when He comes, it will be in power and great glory."

The Sovereign of Israel is indeed coming. But, before then, He will come for His Church. This presents the Christian with a challenge to live in a manner that is worthy. Those outside of Christ are still in the Day of Grace, and can repent of their sin and be saved.

"The Day is at hand of most wonderful glory;
The night of Earth's darkness is now almost past;
The Saviour is coming! Oh, rapturous story!
Soon now shall have dawned the glad day that shall last.

The signs are abundant: the Scriptures foretold them—
Grave, perilous times have assuredly come:
And weapons most awesome (great nations now hold them)
Strike terror in hearts o'er their possible doom.

But Christians—we look for the Saviour from Heaven!
How blessed the hope grows as midnight draws near!
We cannot be blind to the growth of the leaven—
But—looking for Him—will protect us from fear."

J. Danson Smith.

The Jew is indeed a tremendous sign!

CHAPTER 2

THE INTERNATIONAL SIGN

In the Bible we are told in Matthew chapter 24, in Mark chapter 13 and in Luke chapter 21 that "nation shall rise against nation". This is a sign of the last days. We are also told by the Lord Jesus Christ: "Behold the fig tree, and all the trees; When they now shoot forth, ye see and know of your own selves that summer is now nigh at hand" (Luke 21:29, 30). This reference to "all the trees" is surely pointing to the "budding" and "shooting forth" of a vast number of new nations. This very thing has happened in recent times. Since the close of World War Two the former British Empire has been broken up, and many of the territories have been given their independence. Other colonies belonging to other nations have also been given their own self-government. As a result, we have a great number of new nations "bursting forth" and seeking to make their influence felt today. All over the continent of Africa new nations have appeared, and in the West Indies, East Indies and other areas of the world new nations have become established. This certainly is a further sign of our Saviour's return. When these things BEGIN to happen, the Bible says His coming is at hand! So, there is an International Sign which is quite significant.

A. POLITICAL TURMOIL

In Luke chapter 21 verse 25 we read that "There shall be . . . upon the earth distress of nations, with perplexity; the sea and the waves roaring". And, while this verse refers to events just prior to the return of the Lord in glory, we can see that this situation exists already. The national leaders are filled with fear and perplexity. They do not know which way to turn! There is trouble on almost every hand. The "sea and the waves" are indeed roaring!

Dr. Oswald J. Smith writes in his book *Prophecy—What Lies Ahead*: "Men know not which way to turn. Nations are perplexed. Uncertainty characterizes the attitude of every statesman. The future is concealed in obscurity. That a terrible catastrophe lies just ahead is the conviction of all. But what, and from which direction will it come? National selfishness seems to have gripped the entire race. The worst that is in man is now manifesting itself. A spirit of greed and lust dominates human hearts. One wonders if the abyss has not already opened to release its myriads of demons for the ruin of man, both nationally and individually. Be that as it may, thousands, anxious and perplexed, are asking the question, 'What next?' "

One thing is clear! The Saviour's return is at hand!

Dr. W. Graham Scroggie once said: "The inter-relation of the nations is such that the action of one directly or indirectly affects all". That statement is true, for most of the world is in one alliance or another, and political turmoil increases daily. Most nations consult their friends and associates. The Prime Minister of Great Britain is in constant touch with the President of the United States. The Israeli Prime Minister also keeps in constant contact. The black leaders are in frequent discussions regarding their problems. The Far Eastern peoples consult, and, of course, the Communistic countries are under daily control from Moscow and Peking. The nations are indeed greatly disturbed today. "Distress of nations with perplexity" is quite evident today. Many of the world's problems are hard to solve. The political turmoil will continue, and increase!

B. Peace Talks

Another matter concerning the International Sign is the Peace Talks that constantly go on. After World War One the League of Nations was formed to keep world peace. It did not succeed! After World War Two the United

Nations came into being with a determination on the part of many that there should be no more war. Since then, there have been various limited wars—in Korea, Malaya, Vietnam, Congo and elsewhere. World politicians fly backwards and forwards discussing disarmament, control of weapons, and of course "Peace"! The Bible says in I Thessalonians 5:3: "When they shall say, Peace and safety; then sudden destruction cometh upon them".

Dr. M. R. DeHaan in his book *Signs of the Times* says: "A passage like that needs little comment in these days of peace conferences and other organizations which have been set up for the express purpose of bringing world peace. Never before has there been more talk of peace. Yet, never before has there been more fear and threat of war. There are more men under arms throughout the world today than in any other period of so-called peace time in all of the world's history. All we hear is peace, fighting to maintain peace and police protection to preserve peace. At the same time we hear of war and threatenings of war, bickering among the nations, manoeuvring for power, clever manipulations of power politics and a race for spheres of influence throughout the world. The international deliberations of today are following the pattern laid down in the Scriptures for these last days, 'when they shall say, Peace and safety; then sudden destruction cometh upon them'. The Bible clearly states that there can be no lasting world peace until the Prince of Peace, the Lord Jesus Christ, returns."

The peace talks will continue, but the Bible makes it plain that wickedness and strife will increase. There can be no peace until the Saviour returns to reign. Unfortunately, this "peace talk" attitude is affecting our civilisation in other ways, too. There has been a very marked softening in the moral fibre of our society. Criminals are no longer punished suitably, for that would be inhuman! Industrial strikes by trade unions are more frequent and "peace talks" with their leaders are constantly held. Truly, there is no peace!

Dr. John F. Walvoord and his son in their helpful book *Armageddon, Oil and the Middle East Crisis* state that: "The advance of modern technology in communication, transportation, and the weapons of war have suddenly shrunk our world. A missile can reach any part of the world in less than thirty minutes. Television and radio provide instant communication. A world in which men could once live in a measure of isolation is now geographically one. Every major event, whether it is an oil embargo, the development of a new nuclear weapon, or the threat of starvation, creates waves on the sea of mankind and pounds on distant shores. Men and nations can no longer live in isolation. . . . Some form of universal government seems the only hope for a world that can easily destroy itself. The problems facing the world are international problems—nuclear war, overpopulation, starvation, pollution and economic instability."

Yes, indeed the peace talks are part of the international sign.

C. POWER BLOCS

As we look further we notice distinct Power Blocs have emerged in recent times. These are foretold in the Bible, and, while the present Power Blocs may not be exactly the final ones, nevertheless they are on the lines indicated by Scripture. Rev. Ian MacPherson says regarding these Blocs: "The map of Biblical prophecy may be said to be divided into four main sections, corresponding to the four points of the compass, with Israel as centre, thus: (1) The Western Confederacy; (2) the Northern Dictatorship; (3) the Southern Alliance; and (4) the Federation of the Far East. Dogmatically and precisely to identify these power blocs of Biblical prophecy with the great political aggregations of today would be unwarranted and unwise; and yet students of the prophetic Scriptures cannot but be impressed with the correspondence between them. The Western Confederacy would seem to be foreshadowed by the European Community; the Northern Dictatorship (the self-styled 'Dictatorship of the Proletariat') by Russia and her satellites; the Southern Alliance by the United Arab Republic (or the Arab nations); and the Federation of the Far East by China and her minions."

The revival of the Roman Empire is foretold in the Bible. In the Book of Daniel chapter 2, Nebuchádnezzar was given a vision of a great image. Various parts of the body foreshadowed a number of world empires and the final one is shewn in the ten toes: "part of iron, and part of clay" (v. 42). The Apostle John also speaks of this empire in Revelation chapter 13. Verse 1 says: "And I stood upon the sand of the sea, and saw a beast rise up out of the sea, having seven heads and ten horns, and upon his horns ten crowns". Outstanding Bible scholars are all agreed that those passages, and Daniel chapter 7 also, refer to what Dr. C. I. Scofield calls "a confederated ten-kingdom empire covering the sphere and authority of ancient Rome". *The Western Bloc* is surely this—and associated are the United States, and one or two other nations such as Canada, Australia and New Zealand.

The Russian Power Bloc is obvious. "The king of the North" without question is Russia. She, with her satellites, form the Northern Bloc or the Communistic Bloc. It is interesting to note that the giant which slept for hundreds of years has awakened! From being a backward, illiterate land in the early years of this century, it has developed into a world force which could strike terror into the hearts of her enemies. Mr. MacPherson goes on to say: "Let it be mentally noted that the rise of Russia in fifty years from a nation, which, for all its pageantry and literature and music, was comprised for the most part of illiterate peasantry to one of the two leading world-powers, is certainly a very remarkable portent presaging the personal return of Christ."

The third Power Bloc is that of *the Arab world.* Egypt would like to dominate this group, and for years she has sought to do so by leading the Arabs in battle against God's earthly people—Israel. The whole Arab world is bound together by religion—the Islamic religion—and a common hatred of the Jews! Dr. John Wesley White, in *W.W. III*, states: "Working in alliance with Russia will be the rulers of 'the south', a bloc of nations that may roughly coincide with those African countries that banded together in Addis Ababa, Ethiopia, in 1963 to form the Organisation of African Unity. The Bible repeatedly refers to Egypt as the leader. . . . The Bible gives a great deal of attention, prophetically, to Egypt in the time of the end, in terms of her being both blessed and cursed. Militarily, today, Egypt is piling up arms."

The whole continent of Africa today is a picture of seething unrest. Strong Communistic influences are at work. A number of years back the late Colonel Nasser of Egypt fancied himself as head or president of a United States of Africa. It is clear that the Soviets have a major interest in that continent, and they will continue to strengthen their links there. The continent will be somewhat united by the "Arab" factor and by Egypt's leading. The Bible indicates this and specifically names Libya and Ethiopia (Daniel 11:43).

The fourth Power Bloc is that of *China and the Far East*. This, also, is a sign of our Saviour's soon coming! The Bible speaks of "the kings of the East", and in Revelation chapter 9 verse 16 we are told that an army of two hundred million men will advance on Israel from the East. In recent times it has been made public that China today has a huge army, and a militia strength of "two hundred million". She has also for many years been building a highway from China right through to the Middle East. This road is being completed and the way is now open for China to come! Like Russia, she also covets Israel and aims at world supremacy. Already, several East African countries are under China's influence. The Chinese Bloc includes various territories she has conquered or annexed —such as N. Korea, Tibet and other places. China has awakened in recent times from a long slumber to become a major world power! Even the Russian Bloc fears China today. This Bloc is so strong. Also, they are prepared to lose millions of men in their drive for world domination.

Again quoting Dr. Walvoord and his son, they write: "Hundreds of millions of men will be involved in a gigantic world power struggle centred in the Middle East. The area will become the scene of the greatest war of history. Great armies from the south, representing the millions of Africa, will pour into the battle arena. Other great armies from the north, representing Russia and Europe, will descend on Palestine. Climaxing the struggle will be millions of men from the Orient, led by Red China, who will cross the Euphrates River and join the fray. Locked in this deadly struggle, millions of men will perish in the greatest war of all history. This is what the Bible describes as Armageddon. Before the war is finally resolved, and the victor determined, Jesus Christ will come back in power and glory from heaven. His coming, accompanied by millions of angels and saints, is described in graphic terms in Revelation 19. Coming as King of kings and Judge of the world, He will destroy the contending armies and bring in His Own kingdom of peace and righteousness on earth."

The four Power Blocs are obvious and are all in keeping with Bible prophecy! The basic alignments are there today. Surely, these point to the fact that the coming of the Lord for His Own is at hand! Are we ready for the Rapture?

CHAPTER 3

THE RUSSIAN SIGN

"When it is evening ye say, fair weather: for the sky is
red. And in the morning, foul weather today: for the sky
is red and lowring. Ye can discern the face of the sky;
but can ye not discern the signs of the times?" (Matthew
16:2, 3). John Ritchie many years ago said: "There is a
weather-beaten old tag of our childhood days which says:
  'A red sky at night is the shepherd's delight,
  A red sky in the morning is the shepherd's warning.'
That old saying seems to be well-founded and would
appear to have support both from Scripture and science.
Few people were more adept at discerning the face of the
sky than the Jews, and to them the RED DAWN was an
acknowledged sign, as it is with us today, of foul weather
ahead. . . . The 'red dawn' is an expression used in a
political sense in our day, as being the ultimate goal of
the communist and others—the avowed enemies of the
present state of society—of the time when the restraint
of ordered government will no longer thwart their
purposes."

The above passage aptly describes the present world
situation and the growing menace of Russian Communism.
The Red Flag is the Communist's song. Red is their
colour. We speak today of Communists as "the Reds",
and so we are justified in speaking of "the Red Dawn" as a
sign of the Saviour's return.

A. RUSSIA'S DESIRE

The rapid growth of Communism, and its parent
Socialism, has been amazing. Today, more than a third
of the world is in the fiendish control of Communism.
Russia is an atheistic and materialistic nation—determined

to conquer and rule the whole of the world. By every means possible she seeks to disrupt and destroy. Although professing to be "communist"—that is sharing around and making things equal—Russia is an extreme dictatorship and all who resist the dictates of her government are oppressed, imprisoned or liquidated. Russia's desire is power—world domination through communism! The Red menace is growing—rapidly! Dr. Lehman Strauss, in his book *The End of This Present World*, says: "Possibly you were of the opinion that Communism means to share and share alike. No, never! Under Communism a few men rule an entire country. If the United States were overthrown by a communist country, perhaps fifteen or twenty men would rule our country. All industry would be nationalized. All farms would be taken away from their owners. All business enterprises, small and large, would be seized. Insurance companies would be dissolved, so that no American could receive income from any source whatever. This action would be immediate, drastic and without appeal. Then, the country clubs, swimming pools and other 'luxuries' would be used for the benefit of the 'workers'. Now these 'workers' are not the masses who labour in the factories, mines and on farms. They are the Party bosses who work for the Party. Actually they are working for themselves. They subjugate the people, making slaves of them, while they live in luxury. To the Communist, total communisation means state ownership."

Russia's desire for world power is a sign of the Saviour's near return for His Own, for all this is foretold in the prophetic Word. Russia is mentioned as the "king of the north" in the Bible, and in those passages in particular we learn much of what is to happen. In Ezekiel chapters 38 and 39, Daniel chapter 11 verses 40-45 and in Joel chapter 2 verse 20 Russia is clearly defined! "The land of Magog" has long been recognized as Russia. Writers, including Josephus, the first century Jewish historian, and Pliny the Roman historian of early times also, all agree that Magog is Russia.   Russia is a vast country already, but her desire for power is great!   Salem Kirban has given the following statistics: "Russia—the Union of Soviet Socialist Republics—in area the largest country in the world—stretches across two continents from the North Pacific to the Baltic Sea.   It occupies the Northern part of Asia and the Eastern half of Europe.   Its Western borders brush against Finland, the Baltic, Poland, Czechoslovakia, Hungary and Rumania.   On the South it is bounded by Rumania, the Black Sea, Turkey, Iran, Afghanistan, China, Mongolian Peoples Republic, and North Korea.   In the far North-East, the Bering Strait separates it from Alaska.   The vast territory of the U.S.S.R. occupies a sixth of the earth's land surface.   In land area it covers 8,647,172 square miles and has a population of about 250 million people. . . .   The U.S.S.R. is extremely rich in natural resources.   It claims to possess 57% of the world's coal deposits, 58% of its oil, 41% of iron ore, 88% of the manganese, 54% of potassium salts, 30% of phosphates and 25% of all timberland. Gold production is estimated at more than 50% of the production of the rest of the world."

Russian Communism has a world spy network with agents in every land.   Today, in the West, our nations are constantly disrupted by strikes.   Many of these are "engineered" by Russian agents.   This desire for world power will never be fulfilled, for the Bible tells of Russia's end.   At present, our lives are disturbed and upset by the selfishness of strikers and others—but the end of Russian Communism is not far away.   Many today who pose themselves as Socialists are also frequently found to be members of the Communist Party—but the Christian need not fear!   Communism, which is an anti-God system, is heading for destruction!

Russia, in her desire for world power, has developed a fantastic weapons system.   She is probably the most heavily armed country in the world.   Her space program, too, is not so much in aid of science and research, as it is in regard to finding ways of controlling the world from Outer Space.

Dr. J. Dwight Pentecost comforts us by saying: "Russian Communism is absolutely under the authority and control of God and can not go one step beyond that which God purposes. No matter how dark this world situation looks, it has not gotten out from under God's sovereign authority, but God is letting all things progress according to His will. While men think they are developing their plans and purposes, it is all according to God's plans, so that He may demonstrate that He is God without an equal."

B. RUSSIA'S DRIVE

In a not too distant day the forces of Russia and her allies will attack Israel. Ezekiel chapters 38 and 39, as well as Daniel chapter 11 and Joel 2:20—passages which we have already mentioned—adequately describe what will happen. It is absolutely clear that Russia's drive for Israel will be sudden—like a whirlwind! Israel will be dwelling in a measure of peace and safety—no doubt under some guarantee from the Man of Sin who is yet to be revealed. Daniel, in chapter 9 verse 27, says: "He (the Antichrist) shall confirm the covenant with many (Israel) for one week (seven years)".

Richard W. DeHaan affirms: "First, the invasion of Palestine from the north will occur in the 'latter days'. It is in the future. Nothing that resembles this prophecy has ever taken place. We know the 'latter days' of Israel's history will begin when God restores the repentant nation to the centre of His redemptive program. Second, this prophecy will be fulfilled at a time when the Jews are back in the land and feel secure. This is not true of Israel today. The threat of war with her Arab neighbours is real. The nation's armies stand in continual readiness for battle. The predicted feeling of security will prevail only when present enemies become friendly, or when some great world power, feared by all the nations, gives Israel an absolute guarantee of protection."

Russia's drive will be on Israel. That little land is flourishing today. Huge citrus groves produce magnificent fruit which even the Arabs enjoy! The name "Jaffa" does not, of course, appear on the oranges which they eat! The Dead Sea mineral wealth is also tremendous. The fact, however, which is most important is this—Israel is at the Crossroads of the world. It is the centre—the hub—and the affairs of the world centre on this little land. Russia is determined to capture and control Israel, and she will eventually invade this little country when she feels safe. The Bible says that Russia's drive will take place when God's ancient people "dwell safely, all of them" (Ezekiel 38:8). The Bible describes the Russian invasion as coming "like a storm . . . to cover the land" (Ezekiel 38:9). We know something of Russian air-power today. Perhaps this verse speaks of paratroopers coming in vast numbers. Daniel, in chapter 11:40, speaks of the Russian drive "with chariots, and with horsemen and with many ships". Russian tanks—or chariots—have already been used by the Egyptians in their wars against Israel. Then, Russia is known to have millions of the world's finest horses. If used by the famous Cossack soldiers—they could carry an army rapidly over mountainous country and difficult terrain. Dr. M. R. DeHaan some years ago said: "The most recent statistics reveal that Russia owns some 70% of all the horses in the entire world today. In mountainous terrain where heavy artillery cannot go, horses are able to travel with ease. In the mountains of Israel the last battle of Russia will be fought by great cavalry divisions."

The Russian fleet is already busy beyond words in the Mediterranean and other Middle East areas.

Again to quote Salem Kirban—he says: "We find that the Russian forces move into Israel and cover that land completely. They do so overriding the vigorous objections of the West. And with their invasion they bring death and desolation and bloodshed. These armies will come to rob, plunder and spoil the land that previously has been resting so safely under the supposed protection of the Western powers. But God has a purpose in allowing Russia to come to Israel. God will use Russia as the greatest object lesson this world has ever seen—and that object lesson is that no nation can persecute His people and succeed."

C. RUSSIA'S DEFEAT

Russia's defeat is guaranteed! The infallible Word of God declares it! Those who hate God's people—the Jews —suffer, and those who stand by the Jews are blessed. Genesis 12:3 enunciates a principle which never has changed. This was a promise given to Abraham: "I will bless them that bless thee, and curse him that curseth thee". In World War II Great Britain stood by the Jews and God blessed her with victory. Today, Britain and the U.S.A. are playing a double game—trying to be faithful to the Jews, and yet seeking to appease the Arabs by putting various kinds of pressure on Israel. They had better beware!

Russia's defeat will be resounding. The Bible makes it clear that the West only makes a protest. "Sheba, and Dedan, and the merchants of Tarshish, with all the young lions thereof, shall say unto thee, Art thou come to take a spoil?" (Ezekiel 38:13). A mere protest by the West that is all that poor, little, defenceless Israel can expect! However, God is on her side, and it is He Who defeats the armies of Russia! Dr. J. Dwight Pentecost emphasizes that: "God is going to pour out a judgment from heaven that will wipe out Russia and the military might and power of the Russian confederacy. The world is going to have evidence and testimony that God is in sovereign authority over this earth."

It is interesting to note in Ezekiel chapter 38 what happens. God will use an earthquake (v. 19)—so tremendous that the fish in the sea, the birds in the air, and men and animals on dry land will acknowledge God's hand in judgment. In verse 21 we find that the Russians will fight each other—"every man's sword shall be against his brother". Sickness, torrential rain, fantastic hailstones and fire will follow—and the Russian armies will be devastated! It will take seven months for the Israelites to bury the dead. People the world over will see that it is the Lord's doing.

In closing this chapter I quote some challenging words from the pen of Dr. Lehman Strauss: "The rise of Russia is one of the significant signs of the times, which points to the near return of Christ to take His Own out of this world. It is not until after the Church is raptured that the man of sin, the Antichrist, will show himself. It is not until then that the king of the North will strike. There is only one hope for the child of God. It is 'that blessed hope' of Christ's return for His Church (Titus 2:13). ... In the light of these world-shaking events, are you ready for the coming of the Lord?"

CHAPTER 4

THE EUROPEAN SIGN

Age-end federations are a sign of the Saviour's return. We have already mentioned various power blocs. The most important of these is certainly the European power bloc which is foretold in Scripture. This is often referred to as the Revived Roman Empire. Dr. S. Franklin Logsdon, writing about Europe, says: "The present statehood of Israel is a powerful indication of the ending of the age. The ecumenical movement is another. Perhaps equal to either of these is the European Common Market with its many implications. Sir Winston Churchill coined the phrase, 'The United States of Europe'. At least, it is an economic community, a breaking down of national barriers, a getting together on certain common bases. The whole idea is to re-shape the face of Europe. This was attempted by Caesar, by Napoleon, and by Hitler, but their means to this end were not as subtle or as workable as those proposed by the Common Market. They used ammunition; today's promoters use bread. And let it be said that the re-shaping of the face of Europe approximates the kingdom to arise out of the old Roman Empire—the last Gentile power."

The European Common Market certainly foreshadows the final world empire revealed in the books of Daniel and Revelation. The exact plan of the European Common Market is not economic, but POLITICAL union. This has been stated openly by French, German and Belgian politicians.

An unidentified European leader is quoted as saying, "The final aim is political union, and when this end is realized, a genius must be found to head it up".

A. Its Development

In Daniel chapters 2 and 7, as well as in Revelation chapter 13, the European Sign is revealed. References are made to this great kingdom which will have a tremendous influence world-wide.

Dr. Pentecost has stated: "This whole development is attributed to satanic power—Revelation 13:4. As the Roman empire had been the agency through which Satan attacked Christ at His first advent, that empire in its final form will be the agency through which Satan works against the Messiah at His second advent."

The ten toes in Daniel chapter 2 and the ten horns in Daniel chapter 7 and in Revelation chapter 13 would clearly indicate that this final world power will be a ten-kingdom federation of nations. The European Common Market today has nine member countries with Spain and other nations wishing to join. The European Common Market leaders have stated that it will consist of ten nations only, but it is probable that other nations may become associated in some way or other. It is possible, too, that one or two of the existing members of the European Common Market may leave or be put out, and this would open the way for others to join. The fact is that the Common Market is developing fast and its leaders aim to make it a tremendous world power.

Guy Duty in his book *Christ's Coming and the World Church* writes: "The Common Market is fast emerging as an economic and monetary world power, and it is the world's most important trading unit. Europe is moving with greater unity in the Market, and this time with Britain included. This Market now accounts for the largest bloc of international shipping, and it is the largest exporting combine in the world."

B. Its Definition

In the Book of Daniel chapter 2, Nebuchadnezzar, we are told, was given a vision, and in this vision the figure of a man was revealed. From his description God made plain His plan for various world empires, commencing with his own Babylonian empire—the "head of fine gold". Then followed the "breast and arms of silver"—the empire of Medo-Persia. After this came the "belly and thighs of brass"—representing the Greek empire under Alexander the Great. Finally, the Roman Empire is mentioned—"the legs of iron". It is interesting to note that Daniel spent more time with this empire than the first three. Two stages in this empire are clearly defined. First of all there were the two legs—the Eastern and Western empires of Rome which passed into insignificance hundreds of years ago. Afterwards, the feet "part of iron and part of clay" reveal a revival of the Roman Empire— in ten parts or ten nations. Some of these are shown in the Bible as "iron" while others are represented as "clay". In the Revived Roman Empire—whether it be the European Common Market or something similar—five of the nations will be strong—like iron; the other five will be different—like clay!

God is very clear in His infallible Word. He makes no mistakes. We can therefore be sure that His definition of the Revived Roman Empire is accurate and precise! Ten kingdoms—in a European Federation—these are forecast for the time just after the Lord Jesus Christ returns for His Own. Before our eyes today we see the stage being set. Jesus is coming—any moment! How we need to be ready!

C. ITS DESTINY

The destiny of this Revived Roman Empire is to be the final form of world power before the Saviour returns to set up His throne at Jerusalem and reign for a thousand years. There is no shadow of doubt but this final European empire will be tremendously powerful—like concrete—"iron and clay" mixed. Richard W. DeHaan states: "This revived empire will be a western power. At the time of its greatest extent, Rome covered western

Europe, including England, the Middle East, Egypt and North Africa. This gives us good reason to believe that the ten-kingdom alliance of the future will cover these geographical areas, and perhaps include other nations and territories. It will be worldwide in influence and power, according to Revelation 13:1-10. We cannot deny the possibility that the United States, or other nations of the Western Hemisphere, may be part of this end-time empire. Some conclude that because the United States is not specifically named in the prophetic Scriptures, it will be either completely destroyed or a second-rate power when the final confederacy of nations is formed. But this is not necessarily a correct deduction. In view of its alignment with the nations of western Europe, it is quite possible, perhaps even probable, that the United States will play a significant role in the empire dominated by Antichrist. . . . The present alignment of European nations may fit into the prophetic picture, and the Common Market in Europe could be of great significance."

The European Sign is with us today. Can we doubt the fact that the Saviour's return for His Own is at hand?

Many people in Great Britain were upset and disturbed at being pushed into the European Common Market by their rulers. All the major political parties favoured it. To the man in the street it is bad—prices have soared as a result, and they keep soaring. Then, the Britisher is being forced to associate with countries which have been the nation's enemies in times past—Italy, France and Germany. Common logic questions the wisdom of such an association. Perhaps, if the Lord tarries, Great Britain will yet leave this unholy alliance, for she was never fully part of the old Roman Empire. Scotland and Northern Ireland were never conquered by Rome.

The European Common Market came into being as a result of the Treaty of Rome. This we believe is significant. Why was it not the Treaty of London, or Paris, or Bonn—or some other place? The Bible says it is the Roman Empire revived—therefore, it had to be the

Treaty of Rome!   We are living in fascinating days—the end time of the Age of Grace.   The destiny of the European bloc is that of the greatest kingdom in strength —although poorest in quality.   Each world empire since Nebuchadnezzar has deteriorated—from gold to silver, then brass, iron and finally the mixture of iron and clay. This empire of Europe will for a short period rule the world.   Hal Lindsey in *The Late Great Planet Earth* says: "It is interesting to see in history how men have attempted to put together the old Roman Empire.   Charlemagne tried to do this in A.D. 800.   His 'Roman Empire' included what are now the countries of France, Germany, Italy, Holland and Belgium.   Charlemagne was crowned by the Pope as Emperor Charles Augustus.   But his empire was not the ten-nation confederacy of the Scriptures.   Napoleon tried his strutting best to establish his own Roman Empire.   Another Pope, Pius VII, made a tedious trip across the Alps to Notre Dame cathedral in Paris to place an imperial crown on Napoleon, but the new little Caesar snatched the crown from the Pope and put it on himself.   His empire was not the revived Roman Empire either.   And then there was Hitler.   Does anyone doubt that he attempted to put Rome together again? He said his Third Reich would last a thousand years. God had other plans and Hitler lost.   In spite of the vain striving of man, of the bold and infamous conquerors throughout the ages who failed in their human attempts, we are beginning to see the Ancient Roman Empire draw together, just as predicted."

The destiny, then, of the European Federation is to rule the world for a very short period.   Her strength politically and economically will be great.   However, it is the leader or dictator who will really matter.

D. Its Dictator

In Daniel Chapter 7 verse 8 we read "I considered the (ten) horns, and, behold, there came up among them another little horn". Daniel goes on to say this horn or man has "a mouth speaking great things". In Revelation chapter 13 verses 1-8 the apostle John describes the same person and he also says in verse 5: "There was given unto him a mouth speaking great things". These passages describe the dictator or ruler of the Revived Roman Empire. As we shall deal with him in detail in a later chapter we need not say too much at this point, except that he will be a mighty individual, a dynamic personality, and the dictator of most of Europe. Dr. Oswald J. Smith gives us this picture of what is coming: "No statesmen seem able to solve the problems of the day. No government is dealing successfully with the unemployment situation. Men's hearts are already failing them for fear, and everywhere there is perplexity among the nations. Thus it will continue until—in due time, after all others have failed, a man will arise who will settle every problem. He will solve the financial problem. He will deal with unemployment and every man will be given a job. There will be plenty of money and an abundance of work. None will be idle. He will be heralded far and wide as the saviour of the world, the deliverer of humanity. Statesmen will gladly put everything in his hands. Governments will appoint him to supreme positions of authority and power. And he will be big enough for the job! Thus prosperity will return, for all the financial problems of the world will at last be solved: and it will seem as though the Golden Age has been ushered in. He will be the greatest figure the world has ever seen. Men will idolize and worship him. All nations will do him honour. And then —it will be discovered that he is none other than the Antichrist himself."

It may well be that the Saviour's return for His Own and His sudden removal of them will provide funds from the money and property they will leave behind them to clear up international debts and help the world's economy. This man, however, will be dictator and leader for a period during what is known as the coming Tribulation which will last about seven years.   The second half of this seven-year period is known as the Great Tribulation.

Rev. C. W. Wesley Heming once said: "It is all too evident from events now unfolding that democracy has had its day.   It is DICTATORSHIP that is the evil looming upon the world's horizon.   Liberty as we have known it will soon be no more, freedom just a name, and even our identity will be just numbers.   Everything soon will be governed, ordered and directed from one appointed centre. All this corresponds faithfully with the picture given and declared in Revelation 13.   This is a revelation of a true communal state in which no one who does not bear the mark or identity of its ruler can either eat or live.   Persecution and death are its background, and will be the order of the day (Revelation 13:15 and Daniel 11:44)."

Today, Europe awaits this man, but the Lord Jesus Christ must come first for His Church.

E. ITS DESTRUCTION

In Daniel chapter 7 verses 21-27 we read that the dictator of the Revived Roman Empire will prosper for a period until it pleases the Lord to intervene when He returns in power and glory to set up His Own kingdom, and reign with His saints for a thousand years.   Then, the Antichrist and his European kingdom will be destroyed. Verses 26 and 27 say: "But the judgment shall sit, and they shall take away his dominion, to consume and to destroy it unto the end.   And the kingdom and dominion, and the greatness of the kingdom under the whole heaven, shall be given to the people of the saints of the Most High, Whose kingdom is an everlasting kingdom, and all dominions shall serve and obey Him."

The Bible teaches that the armies of the East and West, the North and South, will eventually march on Israel, and the Battle of Armageddon will then take place.   The plain of Megiddo—the crossroads of the world—is ready! Millions of troops will be there, including the armies of the Revived Roman Empire.   At this point the Saviour—the

Lord Jesus Christ—returns with the armies of heaven. Revelation 19 verses 11-14 says: "And I saw heaven opened, and behold a white horse; and He that sat upon him was called Faithful and True, and in righteousness He doth judge and make war. His eyes were as a flame of fire, and on His head were many crowns; and He had a name written, that no man knew, but He Himself. And He was clothed with a vesture dipped in blood: and His name is called The Word of God. And the armies which were in heaven followed Him upon white horses, clothed in fine linen, white and clean." Victory for Christ is immediate, and the world will know Who is Victor! Revelation 19 verses 19 and 20 tell us what happens: "And I saw the beast, and the kings of the earth, and their armies, gathered together to make war against Him that sat on the horse, and against His army. And the beast was taken, and with him the false prophet that wrought miracles before him, with which he deceived them that had received the mark of the beast, and them that worshipped his image. These both were cast alive into a lake of fire burning with brimstone." Destruction and death, and a final destiny in hell await all who are unsaved —without Christ as their own personal Saviour. Today is still the day of salvation if people will but repent of their sin and accept the Saviour. His coming is at hand, for the European Sign says so!

CHAPTER 5

THE ECUMENICAL SIGN

The rapid growth in recent years of the Ecumenical Movement is a further indication that the coming of the Lord is near. Jesus said in Matthew chapter 24 that when we saw things beginning to come to pass His return was at hand. His coming back as King of kings is not far away, but His return for His bride may be at any moment! The Bible foretells, in no uncertain way, this end-time sign, the sign of the Ecumenical Movement.

A. ITS PROGRESS

There has been, this century, an amazing trend towards a common world church. This is known as "the Ecumenical Movement". In 1910 the first move toward this took place in the Edinburgh Missionary Conference. From this beginning there was developed in 1948 what we call the World Council of Churches. The purpose of this movement or organization is the uniting of all churches, and the establishment of a world religious system. Wim Malgo, in *Shadows of Armageddon*, states: "The official church, represented by the Ecumenical Movement, is turning away from the Gospel, away from Jesus Christ the Crucified, towards the political world. . . . Simultaneously, the World Council of Churches strives to become united with the Communists."

From small beginnings, the World Council of Churches has grown quickly. Its stated purposes are "common action, co-operation, and ecumenical consciousness". Today, we see many denominations, which stood apart on various grounds of doctrine or belief, coming together. Their old principles are being abandoned.

Dr. Lehman Strauss made this statement: "The most prominent leaders of the Ecumenical Movement have repeatedly and emphatically stated that their one goal is a united church. They deplore the wild tempest in the churches which has resulted in a disintegration into many small sects which quarrel with one another and condemn each other. They maintain that church unity was broken by selfish and sinful men. And so they appeal for an ecumenical church on the ground of our Lord's statement in His high-priestly prayer, 'that they may be one, even as we are one' (John 17:22). As a matter of fact, those were the words quoted in Latin by the late Pope John when he set in motion the ecumenical wheels of the Roman Church. . . . . But is the unity which the Ecumenical Movement seeks the unity which Scripture teaches? The answer to this question is an emphatic *No!* This modern Ecumenical Movement seeks a union which is organizational, visible and hierarchical, and which ultimately will bring all religions under the authority of Rome. But the unity of believers in Jesus Christ, as taught in the New Testament, is a spiritual unity brought to pass, and made experientially real by the incoming and indwelling of the Holy Spirit."

The World Council of Churches continues to make progress steadily. The principles for which our forefathers fought and died are being forgotten. Freedom of worship, as well as Reformation principles are left aside in the mad rush for a world church system. People are brain-washed into believing that Roman Catholicism with its paganism and idolatry is not so bad after all, and unity with Rome is encouraged. In some places, today, evangelicals are meeting in gatherings of Presbyterians, Anglicans, Baptists, Roman Catholics and others in a desire for unity!

B. ITS PURPOSE

The purpose of the Ecumenical Movement is the establishment of a world church. This will take place. It is probable, however, that the complete union of the churches will not happen until AFTER the coming again of the Lord Jesus Christ for His Own. The Bible calls this united world church "Babylon". In Revelation chapter 17 we have a whole chapter describing the Ecumenical Movement and what is going to happen to it. "Babylon the great, the mother of harlots and abominations of the earth" is the title given to this wicked, monstrous movement. The amazing thing is that many born-again Christians are contented and happy to stay in this system as members of ecumenical churches. The Bible says "Come out from among them, and be ye separate, and touch not the unclean thing" (2 Corinthians 6:17).

The purpose is unity—a united world church, with Rome at its head! The Bible says this will come about, for it well describes the Roman Harlot and all the small harlots in Revelation chapter 17. These churches have played with politicians for power, and in the end will suffer at the hands of the last great politician—the Antichrist. They do not have a Bible base on which to work. Dr. Walvoord and his son show how the situation has changed. They state: "The common agreement of the church for centuries that the Bible is indeed the Word of God has been abandoned by many who claim to be leaders in the church. For the first time, theologians have proclaimed 'God is dead', and atheism has been advanced as an alternative to Biblical faith."

The apostle Paul warned Timothy in his Second letter chapter 4 verse 3 that "The time will come when they will not endure sound doctrine". Peter, also, in his Second Epistle chapter 3 verses 3 and 4 said: "There shall come in the last days scoffers, walking after their own lusts, and saying, Where is the promise of His coming?"

Dr. John F. Walvoord has also said: "The Bible has something very dramatic to tell us about what will happen to this professing church once the rapture of the Church takes place. While, no doubt, there are many sincere and earnest Christians who are supporting the Ecumenical Movement, it is obvious that when the rapture takes place and every true Christian is caught out of the world, those who are merely professed believers will be left behind. The church structure remaining will be without a single born-again Christian. Its clergymen will never have known Jesus Christ; its liberal theology will deny the Word of God. It is obvious that such a church is headed for divine judgment."

The purpose of the World Church is not to propagate the Gospel. Its aims as stated are "the social and economic development of the nations", "a world family of nations", and "the brotherhood of man under the Fatherhood of God". Many in the Ecumenical Movement are opposed to Biblical theology which stresses salvation through the blood of Jesus alone!

C. Its Position

As we look now at its position in prophecy we find the Ecumenical Sign quite apparent. We have already mentioned Revelation chapter 17 which describes the Ecumenical Church and her end. This is today a very clear sign that the Saviour's return for His Own is at hand.

This false church will be firmly established after the Rapture. It is to be headed by the Church of Rome. It is interesting to look into the position of Babylon as described in the Bible. Dr. S. Franklin Logsdon writes: "The Babylon matter is comprehended within three designations: Historical Babylon in Genesis 11; Ecclesiastical Babylon in Revelation 17; and Political Babylon in Revelation 18. These suffer defeat at the hands of Him Who will not tolerate ungodly usurpation of His royal rights and divine prerogatives. Historical Babylon is symbolized by a monumental tower, Ecclesiastical Babylon by a mystical woman, and Political Babylon by a mighty city. The aim seems to be, respectively, to reach heaven, to rob heaven, and to reject heaven. The proposal of the first was a common language; of the second, a common worship; and of the third, a common privilege—one speech, one church, one society. The utopian dream in each instance may be expressed as a cohesion of the people, a commingling of the churches, and a confluence of power—to stay together, to worship together, to excel all others.''

The position in prophecy of the Ecumenical Movement is "in the last days"—so we see it as an end-time sign present with us. The true Church consists of every soul who has repented of their sins, trusted Christ as Saviour and been washed in His precious atoning blood. Not one member of this body will be part of the Harlot Church on the day of its destruction. By God's grace they will be removed any day now from this scene of time. Those who are not yet ready, or perhaps not sure, must now seek to get right with God. The Bible says "Now is the day of salvation" (2 Corinthians 6:2).

Dr. John Wesley White describes the dramatic situation in these words: "This superchurch will become the haven of hundreds of millions of others who will seek spiritual security in it. With the Holy Spirit no longer restraining the mystery of iniquity, this ecumenical ecclesiastical amalgam will bear few resemblances to today's church. . . . Being in alliance with the political powers of the Middle East, this supra-religious organization will work in concert with the emerging Antichrist. This unholy bedfellow arrangement is pictured in Revelation 17, which describes an evil harlot riding a scarlet-coloured beast. For centuries, Bible scholars have been convinced of this significance: the harlot is a religious monster-movement and the beast is the Antichrist. This wicked marriage will be the phalanx of a world sinking to an all-time nadir of immorality.''

D. ITS POWER

We can see from the Bible that the history of Christianity begins with one church, founded on the Day of Pentecost, shortly after the Ascension of the Lord Jesus Christ. The Bible also reveals that it ends with two churches. There is the True Church, and also the Ecumenical Church.

The one will be raptured, the other judged. The true church today lacks power because her members in many cases are lukewarm. They are often taken up with materialism and other earthly matters. The false church is strong and increasing in power.

Rev. Ian MacPherson, in *News of the World to Come*, has written: "When a World Church is in mind it is utterly impossible not to take into cognisance the colossal claims of the Church of Rome. . . . Think of her phenomenal membership. Within her worldwide fold she encloses some 500,000,000 people and over them she exercises despotic sway. From the crib to the crypt and beyond she presides, or professes to preside, over their destinies. For the faithful 'Rome has spoken' proves an end of all strife. Her word is law. Her favour is fortune. Her frown is worse than death. . . . The gloved hand of Catholicism can be discerned behind British broadcasting and in America her control of radio, films, television, is reported to be even more powerful and extensive. It goes without saying that a religious institution of such power and proportions cannot be ignored in any attempt to found a World Church."

The Ecumenical Church may be strong and adding each year to its power, but it is only heaping up judgment for itself. It is becoming more and more ungodly! Dr. Ian R. K. Paisley has well said: "No better description can be given than that of the Bible: 'the cage of every unclean and hateful bird' (Revelation 18:2). The bat of agnosticism, the cuckoo of Anglo-Catholicism, the vulture of Romanism, the kite of modernism, the raven of infidelity, the hawk of hypocrisy, the owl of apostasy and the lapwing of perjury, these unclean birds all find a convenient cage in the World Council of Churches."

E. Its Poison

In Revelation chapter 17 verse 4 we read of the "golden cup in her hand full of abominations". This cup—the cup of poison—is being used today in preparation for the day when the Ecumenical Church will have a tremendous say in the world's affairs. World leaders, rulers, kings and ordinary people will drink of the poisonous cup, and when the Man of Sin is ruling in Europe the Ecumenical Church —Babylon the Great—will use him for her own ends. Dr. J. Dwight Pentecost, describing the Ecumenical Church, says: "This woman, clutching the poisonous cup, is on the Beast, causing the Beast to move so that she can go abroad to bring the poison of her cup to added peoples, and tongues, and nations, and kingdoms, to subject them to her power and authority."

F. ITS PORTION

Briefly, let us look at one more detail concerning the Ecumenical Movement. Its portion is disaster! The Rome-controlled world religious system is bound for destruction. The Word of God says it—therefore it will happen!

To quote again from Rev. Ian MacPherson, he says: "The great World Church of the future is not yet fully formed. When it is, a strong bond will be established between it and the head of the ten-kingdomed western confederacy. They will be the world's premier pair, and the False Prophet will act as Public Relations Officer to the Antichrist and his policies. When the image of the Man of Sin is set up in the Temple at Jerusalem, his aide-de-camp will induce and incite the world to worship it. But eventually they will alter their policy towards the false World Church. Envious of her fabulous wealth or jealous of her imperious authority, they will subject her to utter spoliation. 'The ten horns which thou sawest upon the beast, these shall hate the whore, and shall make her desolate and naked, and shall eat her flesh, and burn her with fire' (Revelation 17:16)."

The next prophetic event in God's program, as revealed in His infallible Word, is the Rapture—or snatching away of the True Church before the awful horrors of the Tribulation take place. The Bible says "Be ye also

ready"—to the true Christian—that he may live worthily
—and to the unsaved soul that he may put his trust in
Christ and not in the church.   The Ecumenical Sign is
here!

"He is coming!   He is coming!   Yes, the certainty grows
    bright!
His voice shall sound love's summons—at morn, or noon,
    or night!
How blest if we are ready, through sovereign grace, to go,
And, unashamed, shall meet Him, and His wondrous
    welcome know."

                                    J. Danson Smith.

Chapter 6

THE NUCLEAR SIGN

Yet another sign of the soon coming of the Lord Jesus is that of the nuclear age. In the course of the last generation or two a whole new system of weaponry has been devised. For centuries the nations depended for safety on military man-power—hoping by such strength to out-number and defeat the enemy. Then came some exciting advances in technology. Rifles were replaced with machine-guns. Tanks, armoured vehicles and other land weapons came along, while in the air fighters and bombers became vital. Towards the end of World War Two scientists invented "flying bombs", and then giant rockets with destructive warheads. Finally, the Atomic Bomb was produced and its delivery upon Japan caused the surrender of that country and the end of the war.

Guy Duty has said: "Satan is bringing the nations to the brink of destruction. Military experts tell about the horrible possibility of nuclear World War Three during the next few years, and they give frightful descriptions of hundreds of millions dying in the first attack. This is favourable to Satan's peace plan as he skilfully weaves his net around the world. What nation would reject a peace plan that would save the world from nuclear destruction?"

"Peace at any price" may be a tempting slogan in view of the ghastly consequences which would come with a nuclear war, but peace cannot and must not be accomplished this way. The Communists would like to break down the West with fear—fear of bombing, fear of destruction, fear of the holocaust of a nuclear war. The nuclear age is surely another sign that the Saviour's return is near.

The nuclear weapons today have ranges covering the

whole world. No longer do they require men to deliver the bombs by plane. By the pressing of a button rockets are launched carrying nuclear warheads which would unleash death and destruction in untold measure.

The born-again person need not fear a nuclear war for the return of the Lord Jesus Christ must take place soon. The destruction caused by atomic, hydrogen or neutron bombs, or other nuclear devices, would be so colossal that Scripture would almost certainly mention it, and the only devastating happenings recorded in Scripture as still in the future refer to the Great Tribulation when God's judgments will be poured out on a Christ-rejecting earth.

Evangelist Gavin Hamilton, in his book *The Rapture and the Great Tribulation* says: "It is interesting to note that General Douglas MacArthur said, 'We have had our last chance. The battle of Armageddon is next'. What zero hour holds for the world of mankind is vividly described by Professor Harrison Brown. He says, 'If the hydrogen bomb works, technically speaking, it is easy to visualize a series of hydrogen bomb explosions carried along a North-South line at about the longitude of Prague. The radio-activity produced by the explosion would be carried Eastward by the winds, destroying all life within a strip fifteen hundred miles wide, extending from Leningrad to Odessa, and three thousand miles deep, extending from Prague to the Ural Mountains. The United States could be attacked in similar manner. Hydrogen bomb explosions could be set off on a North-South line in the Pacific approximately a thousand miles off California reaching there in about a day, and New York in four or five days, killing all life as it traversed the continent.' "

Many different nuclear weapons are being manufactured today. Many different nations are involved. Russia, China, U.S.A., Great Britain, France and a considerable number of other educated and scientific nations are continually spending vast sums of money in nuclear research. In the Second World War twenty one million were killed in battle; between fifteen and twenty million more were killed in air-raids; twenty-nine and a half million were wounded and a hundred and fifty million were left homeless. In a nuclear war, lasting perhaps but a few hours or days at the most, a far greater number would be killed, injured and made homeless. The child of God must "look up" for "the coming of the Lord draweth nigh". We are not to be depressed or worried about nuclear war. The nuclear age is a sign of our Saviour's return. Luke 21 verse 28 says: "When these things begin to come to pass, then look up, and lift up your heads; for your redemption draweth nigh".

When one speaks of "nuclear war" the thought of the atomic bomb springs to mind. This word "atomic" occurs once in the New Testament although our English translations have not used it. Professor John C. Banks has said: "The word 'atomic' is an adjective, and it means 'That which cannot be cut'—that is, something indivisible, something so very small that it cannot be cut or divided into smaller parts. . . . In 1 Corinthians 15:52 we have the showing or the declaration of a mystery. We are informed that we shall all be changed (that is the members of the Body of Christ) . . . 'In a moment' . . . and there you have the Greek word 'atomic'! That is to say, in a fraction of time so small that it cannot be split, in one dazzling moment, we shall be changed! We shall put on immortality, incorruption, and the age of grace as we know it will be over! There will be no advance advertisement as the world is accustomed to have it. There will be no advance agent, as the world knows such, to prepare town after town, city after city, county, state or country. There will be no preliminary 'come-in' advertisements to get people ready. It will be all over 'in a moment', in a fraction of time so small that it cannot be divided any farther."

Today is the day of salvation. The Bible makes it clear that men and women, boys and girls must repent of their sins now and trust the Saviour while they may. Soon, the Day of Grace will be through. The message is simply and clearly stated in these lines of my father:

> "Only today is the day of salvation,
> Only today is God's offer to you.
> Only today is the great invitation—
> Will you take Christ—today?"

J. Danson Smith.

Oh, that people would heed this call!

In 2 Peter chapter 3 verse 10 the great apostle speaks of "the day of the Lord", and he says "the heavens shall pass away with a great noise, and the elements shall melt with fervent heat, the earth also and the works that are therein shall be burned up". This would seem to be a perfect description of a nuclear explosion causing total world-wide destruction and devastation. This passage, and other similar ones in the Old Testament, until recent times must have sounded fantastic to many, although the Bible-believing Christian knows that what God states in His infallible Word will take place! The earth was once cleansed by water at the Flood. It is yet to be cleansed by fire AFTER the Millennium. Years ago, it seemed impossible for a world with so many oceans and so much water to go on fire—yet, today, we know it is a possibility —thanks to nuclear fission!

Dr. M. R. DeHaan, writing of the atom, says: "Scientists have warned us that man now is in possession of knowledge concerning atomic and cosmic energy which may well result in the destruction of this entire world. This age will go down in history as the atomic age, the age in which man, by God's permission, has solved the secret of the universe, and now has in his hands a power by which, if God would permit it, completely to destroy himself and the world. . . . According to Peter's words in the Scripture we read man will not learn his lesson. According to the Word of God, this world will not continue in its present form for ever, for God plainly says that there is a day coming when 'the heavens shall pass away with a great noise, the elements shall melt with fervent heat, the earth also and the works that are therein shall be burned up' (2 Peter 3:10). The word for 'earth' in this verse is 'ge', the word used not for the world of men but for the material earth, consisting of the soil and the physical elements. This, says God, is going to be burned up with everything in it."

For those outside of Christ the future is indeed dark and gloomy. The final destruction of the world by fire is yet a long way off—but in the near future there will be terrible destruction—in the Great Tribulation period. Oh, how wonderful it is that a loving God sent His only-begotten Son to make a way of escape for sinners!

The nuclear weapons today are causing frequent peace conferences. The talk is of "peace, peace, when there is no peace" (Jeremiah 6:14). Such talks will continue—as men know what nuclear war will mean. Professor Walvoord in *The Church in Prophecy* has stated: "Millions of intelligent people today believe that the only hope of averting atomic suicide is to accept some form of international control in which individual nations will surrender some of their sovereignty in favour of international control. . . . In a world brought close together by rapid means of travel and weapons of destruction which can reach any portion of the globe, the significant fact is that for the first time in history the concept of a world government has seized the minds of large masses of people. The world situation with its scientific improvements has developed to the point where such a world government becomes a necessity if future world conflicts should be avoided."

We see today a willingness for world control—yet another sign of the times! It is interesting to note that the Bible mentions "wars and rumours of wars" (Matthew 24:6) as an end-time sign! This fear of war is going to remain—until finally the Prince of Peace sets up His Millennial Kingdom, and keeps down all trouble. Nuclear weaponry causes much of this fear. As Hal Lindsey has said: "Man cannot stop war because he will not accept the basic reason and cause for war—nor will he accept the cure for this basic cause. God says: 'From whence come wars and fightings among you? come they not hence, even of your lusts that war in your members? Ye lust, and have not: ye kill, and desire to have, and cannot obtain: ye fight and war, yet ye have not' (James 4:1, 2). Inside of man there is a selfish, self-centred nature. This is the source of what God calls sin. Sin is basically self-centred seeking and striving—going our own way, with our backs turned on God. It is because of this selfish nature with which we were born that we cannot have consistent peace with ourselves, our family, our neighbours, or, on a broader scale, with other nations."

So, wars and especially the danger of nuclear war will remain—until the Battle of Armageddon when Christ will return in power and glory to reign. The nuclear age is certainly a sign of the Saviour's return!

"Momentous days are on us! Our eyes may soon behold
A mighty clash of nations which prophets have foretold;
A clashing and a cleaving of unmatched magnitude,
Wrought by some super-being with evil power endued.

Momentous! Yes, momentous! But shall we be afraid?
The mighty conflict cometh, yet may our hearts be stayed!
The Lord from Glory cometh—His Coming draweth nigh;
Earth's most colossal conflict we'll see yet from on high.

The nations all are arming! The worst is yet to be!
For Armageddon cometh, not far from Galilee;
But brothers, Christian brothers, fear not of being there;
Before that awful carnage, Christ cometh to the air.

The days of tribulation are truly near at hand;
'Perplexity of nations' e'en now invades each land;
Yet, not for woes and terrors, and earth's onrushing night
Look we for, but the Morning of cloudless glory bright."

J. Danson Smith

CHAPTER 7

THE SATANIC SIGN

In recent times there has been a remarkable growth of interest in the occult. Along with this there has also been greatly increased Satanic activity. This, we believe, is because the devil and his angels know that their time is short and that the Saviour's return for His Own is near. The Bible says in 2 Thessalonians chapter 2 verse 7: "The mystery of iniquity doth already work: only He Who now letteth (restraineth) will let (restrain), until He be taken out of the way." This passage of Scripture teaches plainly that the activity of Satan is at present somewhat restricted by the presence of the Holy Spirit. He is the "Hinderer" or "Restrainer", and He is here on earth to woo and to win a bride for the Lord Jesus Christ. He is the One Who indwells the hearts of all who put their trust in Christ as Saviour, and when the trumpet sounds and the Bride of Christ is "caught up to meet the Lord in the air" the Holy Spirit will go too in order to present the Bridegroom with His blood-washed Bride. Until that moment, Satan's agents will work harder than ever to hinder God's work.

Peter J. Pell has said: "Sinister forces of evil are at work in the world. They were active in Paul's day. These activities are increased an hundredfold today. They will be strengthened in time to come and speedily reach the fearful climax. Satan has his programme, he has set his goal.... Dark as the shadows are, the night will be darker. Awful apostasy marks the end of this age."

Some people seem to doubt the existence of Satan, but all who are involved in the Lord's work are aware of his reality, and his deadly opposition to the Gospel.

John Ritchie helpfully says: "When we turn to the Word of God we find, not perhaps all we should like to know, but all we are intended to know of this strange and mysterious personage whose history is so closely interwoven with that of the human race. His existence, his personality, his power, his purpose, and his future are so plainly written on the sacred page that I have no hesitation in avowing there is as much convincing evidence for the existence of Satan as there is for the existence of God Himself."

The Bible tells us that Satan was a created being—Ezekiel chapter 28:15—and that he was created perfect. He was, however, a free moral agent and through pride he fell—Isaiah chapter 14 verses 12-15. He and the angels that rebelled with him were cast out of heaven and await their eternal doom in the lake of fire—Matthew chapter 25 verse 41.

The increase in Satan's activity today is quite noticeable. He knows he is defeated, for the Cross of Christ smashed his plans. Christ paid in full the penalty for sin and rose from the dead as proof that His death was sufficient. The Bible says in 1 Corinthians chapter 15 verses 20-22: "But now is Christ risen from the dead, and become the firstfruits of them that slept. For since by man came death, by man came also the resurrection of the dead. For as in Adam all die, even so in Christ shall all be made alive." The Cross was no defeat for the Lord Jesus Christ. It was a mighty victory! When He hung there in suffering and shame, before He gave up His life—for He did it voluntarily, for He could not be killed—He shouted "Tetelestai" which in English is the word "finished". The Lord Jesus was not finished, but His work of redemption was! All Satan can do now is to hinder and lead men astray.

The authors of the book *Armageddon, Oil and the Middle East Crisis* make this startling statement: "A generation ago it would have seemed inconceivable that any large number of people in a modern society would believe in spirits and demons, except for Christians who accepted the existence of spirit beings on the testimony of Scripture. What was unthinkable a generation ago is widely accepted today, even on the part of those who have no regard for the Bible. . . . The entire trend toward experimentation with unseen spirits, often aided by drugs, is a frightening example of satanic deception. All these things are an amazing development following the pattern outlined in the prophetic Word for the time of the end. With Christian faith and morality being discarded by many, the new trend toward spiritism and the occult is an obvious satanic substitute for biblical Christianity."

The Bible says in 1 Timothy chapter 4 verse 1 "that in the latter times some shall depart from the faith, giving heed to seducing spirits, and doctrines of devils (demons)". This growth of spiritism is unquestionably a sign of the last days—a sign that the Saviour's return is very near. On every hand today we see the rapid growth of evil, immorality, sex-perversion, drug-taking and open sin. In Great Britain there are vast numbers of witches and warlocks, and their covens are to be found in many places. There is today an uncanny interest in books and films about the devil. The same can be said of America, too, and other countries.

Dr. John Wesley White, writing about Satan, says: "The devil wants much more than recognition of his existence and powers in contemporary society. He wants people to be his. Some ask: 'Does the devil believe in conversion?' Indeed he does. He wants people to give themselves over completely to his charge. Those who do, he strives to make over into ideal representatives of his. As the *New York Times* points out, 'hundreds of thousands of witches' confess to having made 'compacts with Lucifer', having 'traded their immortal souls to Satan'. Millions, in all walks of life, are doing just this today, some of them being in the top echelons of society. Satan prefers his disciples to appear successful."

In Ephesians chapter 6 verse 12 the Christian is warned

of the presence of satanic beings. Paul says—"We wrestle not against flesh and blood, but against principalities, against powers, against the rulers of the darkness of this world, against spiritual wickedness in high places (the heavenlies)". Thank God, the believer in Christ can be armed for this warfare. The weapons and armour are described in Ephesians chapter 6 verses 13-18: "Wherefore take unto you the whole armour of God, that ye may be able to withstand in the evil day, and having done all, to stand. Stand therefore, having your loins girt about with truth, and having on the breastplate of righteousness; And your feet shod with the preparation of the gospel of peace; Above all, taking the shield of faith, wherewith ye shall be able to quench all the fiery darts of the wicked. And take the helmet of salvation, and the sword of the Spirit, which is the word of God: Praying always with all prayer and supplication in the Spirit, and watching thereunto with all perseverance and supplication for all saints." The precious blood of Christ is the Christian's protective covering.

The Satanic influence is not always apparent. In Paul's day the Galatian church was influenced by him, for the Apostle wrote in his letter to them: "O foolish Galatians, who hath bewitched you, that ye should not obey the truth" (Galatians 3:1). Guy Duty explains: "This 'bewitched' is a strong word and it signifies 'fascination', or to be brought under the spell of evil. The serpent had charmed them with false teachers who drew them away from the truth about Christ crucified. . . . The apostle John told us about 'the spirit of error', and there is a spirit that goes with false teaching. Eve was deceived with it. The Corinthians were in danger of becoming beguiled with it, and the Galatians had been bewitched with it. And 'the doctrine of Balaam' which led to covetousness and fornication had corrupted the Pergamos church. This leaven was also working through the prophetess Jezebel in the Thyatira church to 'teach and seduce' the people to commit spiritual fornication—

see Revelation 2:14-23.''

As we survey the world situation today we are aware of the Satanic sign—this rapidly growing interest in Satan and the occult. This, certainly, is a sign of the times, and we recall the words of the Saviour Himself in Matthew chapter 16 verse 3: "Can ye not discern the signs of the times?" The apostle Paul warned us that "in the last days perilous times shall come" (2 Timothy 3:1). Our newspapers constantly reveal atrocities and cruel happenings, and back of all these is Satan—the master of lies, the arch-deceiver, and permanent enemy of God and His people. In many cities, it is unsafe to walk the streets alone in the evenings. The courts of our land have become lenient with sadistic monsters who attack, injure and sometimes kill innocent people. We are indeed in "perilous times"!

Hal Lindsey, in *Satan is Alive and Well on Planet Earth*, asks the question: "Are we in a new age of Satan? Many people would be revolted by the so-called churches which openly worship Satan. . . . Satanic cults are expanding in every major city in the United States. 'We have received reports from other California cities which shew the existence of three Satanist groups in Berkeley, two of them communes, one in Big Sur, one in Venice, five in San Francisco and one in San Diego. The number of Satanist circles gathering in Los Angeles County is indeterminate.' In Europe Satanic masses are held in ruined churches and monasteries, but we should not be deceived by creaking castles or shadowy figures in musty rooms. Satanism is not just an old-world phenomenon. . . In the 'churches' entangled in Satan worship the rites are opposite from those of a Christian church. The world is groaning with its problems. Hearts are crying with their needs. How can anyone bear to live today without Christ? If you know Him, does your very being ache for those who do not? If you know Him, are you living on a note of triumph?"

In closing this chapter, one must make mention of the

apostle Paul's warning to the Church at Corinth in his second Epistle chapter 11 verses 3 and 4: "I fear, lest by any means, as the serpent (Satan) beguiled Eve through his subtilty, so your minds should be corrupted from the simplicity that is in Christ. For if he that cometh preacheth another Jesus, whom we have not preached, or if ye receive another spirit, which ye have not received, or another gospel, which ye have not accepted, ye might well bear with him."

Rev. John Douglas, in *The Charismatic Movement* explains: "Three times over in this verse we have the word 'another'. Mark each occurrence carefully because this is what Paul fears. There is a threefold manifestation of the devil's deception possible: another Jesus, another spirit, another gospel. The modern ecumenical movement, which is being helped on by the charismatic tongues speaking experience, presents all three features of this devilish deception. Theirs is not the Christ of the Bible, nor the Gospel of the Bible. But the devil's purpose is not only to counterfeit Christ and the gospel, he also counterfeits the Spirit and His work and gifts. A look at verse 14 shows us the way in which he does this: 'And no marvel: for Satan himself is transformed into an angel of light'. As an angel, he has power to communicate. As an angel of light, he has power to communicate spiritual sensations. He communicates spiritual sensations by counterfeiting the Holy Ghost. The ecumenical Charismatic movement is just such a counterfeit."

Yes, indeed, Satan will counterfeit the things of God, discredit the Word of God, and attack the child of God! But, we praise God that the Cross of Jesus saw him defeated. The words of P. P. Bliss in his hymn rejoice our hearts when we sing them:

> "Fierce and long the battle rages,
>   But our help is near;
>   Onward comes our great Commander,
>   Cheer, my comrades, cheer!

'Hold the fort, for I am coming!'
Jesus signals still;
Wave the answer back to heaven,
'By Thy grace we will!' "

CHAPTER 8

THE ECONOMIC SIGN

A. FOOD

In the beginning, when God made the earth, everything was beautiful. There were no deserts and there was no bad ground and no waste land. There were no weeds, no pests, no vermin and no disease. These things came into being because of Adam's sin. Genesis chapter 3 verses 17 and 18 says: "Cursed is the ground for thy sake; in sorrow shalt thou eat of it all the days of thy life; Thorns also and thistles shall it bring forth to thee". Several thousand years have passed, and man still fights these products of sin. In fact, today the struggle is greater than ever, for the world's population has become enormous! With growing numbers of people more food is required. Specialists are employed by many governments in their efforts to increase the world's food supply, and yet weeds and disease, and vermin and pests are on the increase. The world today faces a major economic problem, and that problem will be solved only when the Lord Jesus Christ comes back to reign. The Bible says in Romans chapter 8 verses 19 to 22: "For the earnest expectation of the creature waiteth for the manifestation of the sons of God. For the creature was made subject to vanity, not willingly, but by reason of him who hath subjected the same in hope. Because the creature itself also shall be delivered from the bondage of corruption into the glorious liberty of the children of God. For we know that the whole creation groaneth and travaileth in pain together until now." Before then, the Saviour will come for His Own. After He comes back to reign the world conditions will change. Nature will "be delivered" and will return to its former estate.

Today, however, we have this great Economic Sign pointing to the fact that Christ must come soon! Otherwise—only disaster and death face mankind. Guy Duty, in his book *Escape from the Coming Tribulation*, points out that: "Industrial nations, anxious to protect their foreign markets, have been weakened by competitive nations who seek to strengthen their trading positions. The result has been a world chain reaction of competitive reprisals. The world-trade sign is taking shape. International trade is important to world prosperity because it is related to the economic and monetary problems of the nations. Even the United States with all its natural resources is dependent on other nations for large imports of basic raw materials. Dramatic changes are in the making. A unified Europe will come, and a booming international trade. The rush is on in American and foreign shipyards. to build the superships and supertankers. The big industrial nations say they cannot get them fast enough. Shipping experts say this is 'the supertransport era'. For more details read Revelation chapter 18."

B. Oil

Another Economic pointer is that of Oil. This is a commodity vitally needed by every modern nation. It has been in increasing demand ever since the last war, but in recent times it was discovered that only limited reserves were left. Dr. Walvoord and his son in their book on oil state: "The rapid increase in consumption of energy throughout the world has been noted by experts for years, but warnings of an impending crisis fell largely on deaf ears. In industry oil had proved to be cheaper and easier to use than coal. Much of the electrical generating capacity of the United States, especially in the East, depended upon energy derived from oil. In addition, ecologists had pointed out the air pollution caused by coal, particularly by the lower grades of coal which were economically feasible for industrial use. . . . The prospect of limited supplies of gasoline (petrol) threatened the life style as well as the economic prosperity of the United States. Europe and Japan were even more dependent on oil from outside sources, and the threat of limited oil produced panic unprecedented since the days of World War II."

Much travel today depends upon oil. Cars, buses and planes all use this valuable commodity. It is understandable, therefore, that there is a measure of alarm and concern at this economic problem. Shortage of fuel would create a vast number of other problems. The Arab nations, which for centuries were largely sleepy and lazy, have suddenly awakened and they have "cashed in" on this oil crisis and now hold a gigantic share of the world's wealth. Other nations are urgently hunting for new oil supplies, for without oil they could quickly become bankrupt and powerless. Scotland is one area where off-shore oil supplies have been discovered.

C. PLEASURE

In describing the "last days" the Lord Jesus Christ said in Matthew chapter 24 verse 7 that "there shall be famines, and pestilences, and earthquakes, in divers places". Today we read in the press of these things taking place. The Saviour, however, did not say that such conditions would be world-wide. He said that they would occur in different places. In other parts, today, away from the famine areas, there is a tremendous emphasis on pleasure. The keen Christian derives his pleasure from God's Word, and from keeping company with the people of God—those who are separate from the world and its ways, and who seek to live holy lives. The unsaved—all who have never trusted the Lord Jesus Christ as their own personal Saviour—find their pleasure in sin. The world today is pleasure mad and exceedingly sinful. Many people have one chief interest—eating, drinking and taking no thought for the future. This was mentioned by the Saviour as a sign of His return in Matthew chapter 24 verses 37 to 40. Drunkenness is fast on the increase. The love of money,

too, is most apparent.   Trade union leaders are constantly
nagging for more and more money—despite the fact that
the so-called "working classes" are today's rich!

Dr. John Wesley White has said in relation to the
subject before us: "Before Christ returns, whole cultures
will be caught up in a combination of an obsession with
wealth, pleasure madness, and intemperance that will
involve gluttony and drunkenness. . . .   It will be a time
when there will be plenty of people with plenty of money—
for a while—but with the apocalyptic events happening
all around and the impending collapse of society nagging
at them, they will worry about their insecurities and this
will drive them to drink. . . .   Alcoholism (which plagues
ten million Americans) is a chief contributing factor to
seventy-five per cent of the divorces, sixty per cent of
the fatal automobile accidents, fifty per cent of the
homicides, and one third of the suicides.   The National
Institute on Alcohol Abuse and Alcoholism reckons that
alcoholism currently costs Americans forty billion dollars
per year, enough money to feed all the people around the
world who are starving to death.   What is perhaps most
tragic is that the very young are drinking as they never
have before."

D. GAMBLING

One of the trends in recent decades has been the growth
of gambling.   This is caused by the desire of man to obtain
wealth without working for it.   The command of God to
Adam has been forgotten, but Genesis chapter 3 verse 19
still stands: "In the sweat of thy face shalt thou eat
bread"!   Man must work!   Unfortunately governments
sometimes encourage gambling.   Rev. Ian MacPherson
asks the question: "Is there anything in the New Testament to warrant the conclusion that wealth without work
will be a sign of the times of the Second Coming of the
Lord?   Well, quite obviously, we must not expect to find
in the pages of Holy Writ a detailed foreshadowing of the
complex system of present-day gambling.   But James

does speak of those who 'heap up treasure for the last days' (chapter 5:3).''

E. UNEMPLOYMENT

Many countries around the world have vast numbers of unemployed people. Thousands of young people, leaving school, find it difficult to obtain work. This is partly because governments and trade unions have insisted on "juniors" being paid high wages. Any serious employer, therefore, naturally prefers to employ someone with experience for a fraction more. Unemployment is on the increase, and it will continue to grow as machines take over jobs formerly done by people.

Again, Mr. MacPherson asks: "Is mass unemployment itself perhaps a social sign of Christ's Second Coming? There are those who believe it is, and the Biblical passage on which they base that assumption is Zechariah's description of things at the close of this age: 'For before these days there was no hire for man, nor any hire for beast' (ch. 8 v. 10)."

F. THE FUTURE

Controls—national and international—are on the way. Many countries already have them and suffer from them. A world economic solution is planned. Hal Lindsey was up-to-date when he wrote: "Economic manipulations can be used to centralise control in the hands of a few; industry taken from the free market economy and placed under state control; destruction of individual initiative through excessive taxation; regulatory laws which strangle private enterprise; government intervention into every aspect of private affairs. A future world ruler will have his stage set if a one-world economic system is within his grasp."

Although many nations today are on the brink of disaster, in the very near future their economic problems will be solved—temporarily! The Antichrist is coming to power soon, and he will solve in a short-term way the economic ills of the present day.

Dr. John Wesley White, speaking of the future, says: "In spite of the sicknesses and disparities in the economics of the world, or perhaps because of them, there has been a definite trend toward looking more and more toward unification and a central authoritarianism in economics. The International Monetary Fund and the World Bank have been playing an even larger and more widening role in the precarious battle of balancing the international monetary movements, which at times have looked like a zigzag cardiogram after a human heart attack. Of course, the most dramatic post-World War II development in international frontiersmanship in the economic realm . . . is the European Common Market. Out of ten such nations the Antichrist will arise and from this base will launch toward world conquest, until, in-so-far as the economic realm is concerned, he will seize a universal mandate of dictatorship that will galvanize all commerce into a centrally computerized control."

Revelation chapter 13 describes the Antichrist and in verse 8 we read: "All that dwell upon the earth shall worship him". This person is at hand—but the Bible says he will not be revealed until after the Saviour has come for His Own blood-washed people. See 2 Thessalonians chapter 2 verses 7 and 8. The Bible predicts that things will "wax worse and worse". That is the immediate prospect—except for all who are saved and looking for their Saviour from heaven!

> "Deeper still will grow earth's darkness—
> Still more awesome grows its night,
> But for Christ our eyes are looking,
> Quick may come the Rapture bright!"
>
> J. Danson Smith.

CHAPTER 9

THE BEAST SIGN

In concluding the last chapter we mentioned that the coming of the Antichrist was at hand. He is "the beast" referred to in Revelation chapter 13 verses 1-10 as well as in various chapters of Daniel. Chapters 7 and 8 of Daniel refer to him as a "little horn . . . speaking great things". This "little horn" is an end-time sign. In Daniel chapter 7 the various world empires through history are mentioned —Babylon, Medo-Persia, Greece, Rome and finally the Revived Roman Empire under the Beast—the "man of sin" as the Bible also calls him.

As we saw in chapter 4 the European Sign is already here in the shape of the European Common Market. This foreshadows man's final world empire. Politicians are already talking of "political union", and many are looking for a super-man to lead and control. Some years ago Pastor James F. Hardman wrote: "With the international relationships in a state of tension and chaos, it is suggested by some that the need of the hour is a superman who can steer the world into a haven of peace. Upon this point, the words of P. H. Spaak, former Premier of Belgium, in an article upon world conditions in 'Le Soir' are interesting. He wrote, 'The truth is that the method of international committees has failed. What we need is a person, someone of the highest order, of great experience, of great authority, of wide influence. Let him come, and let him come quickly . . . one who will cut out all the red tape, shove out of the way all the committees, wake up the peoples, and galvanise all governments into action. Let him come quickly, this man we need and for whom we wait.' "

The true Christian, of course, knows that there will only

be One Person Who can fully control things—the Lord Jesus Christ—when He comes to reign as King of kings and Lord of lords.   Isaiah chapter 9 verses 6 and 7 remind us of this: "Of His government there shall be no end". However, the Bible also states in 1 John chapter 2 verse 18: "Antichrist shall come . . . it is the last time".

Let us think first of all about the Beast Sign—in relation to a Person.

A. THE PERSON

The Person of Antichrist is not yet known.   The Bible gives him various titles as we have already noted.   He will, we are told, be a remarkable person.   The dragon (Satan) is to endue him with power and with great authority.   He will fascinate the world in a remarkable way.   John says in Revelation chapter 13 verse 3: "All the world wondered after the beast".   The world will go madly after him and will worship him.   See Revelation chapter 13 verses 3 to 8.

Rev. Ian MacPherson, in *News of the World to Come,* makes the following comparisons between Christ and Antichrist: "For weal or woe, the world today waits to welcome the best of men and the worst of men.   Christ is coming!   Antichrist is coming!   And it is immensely significant that in the original the New Testament uses the same term for both advents.   It speaks of the Parousia of Christ and of the Parousia of Antichrist. Here is its reference to the former: 'The coming of the Lord draweth nigh' (James 5:8); and here is its allusion to the latter: 'Then shall that Wicked be revealed whose coming is after the working of Satan with all power and signs and lying wonders' (2 Thessalonians 2:8, 9).   'The devil,' says Martin Luther, 'is God's ape.'   Satan is the master-copyist of the cosmos.   His age-long policy is to counterfeit and caricature the divine.   He is a specialist in the spurious, an expert in fraud, fake, forgery.   Of everything the Almighty is and does he is the impious imitator.   It is an astounding exercise to examine the points of parallel between Christ and Antichrist. Christ is 'the Son of Man'—(John 12:34 etc.). Antichrist is 'the man of the earth' (Revelation 13:11). Christ is 'the Good Shepherd' (John 10:14). Antichrist is 'the idol shepherd' (Zechariah 11:17). The duration of Christ's public ministry was three and a half years: the period during which Antichrist will be at his pernicious prime will be three and a half years. As to the nature of their respective activities, of Christ Acts 2:22 reports that it consisted of 'miracles and wonders and signs'; of the activities of Antichrist the N.T. uses much the same terms: 'power and signs and lying wonders' (2 Thessalonians 2:9). Christ was 'wounded for our transgressions' (Isaiah 53:5): of Antichrist Revelation 13:12 speaks as 'the first beast, whose deadly wound was healed'. And, before Christ reigns in Jerusalem, Antichrist will reign there, just as Saul, the people's choice, ruled before David—the Lord's choice."

Who is this Person? Some have said that the Pope was the Antichrist. Others have said that Napoleon, Hitler, Stalin, Mussolini and others were possibly the Antichrist. But, none of these are. He is Satan's special agent—the second person of the trinity of evil. The other two are Satan himself who counterfeits God the Father, and the False Prophet who counterfeits God the Holy Spirit. This evil Person is the counterfeit of the Lord Jesus Christ, and he will not be revealed until after the Rapture of the Church.

B. THE PEOPLE

This war-weary world of ours is looking for a world leader—a man who will give them peace and prosperity, and when the Beast is revealed they will worship him, and adore him, and say: "Who is like unto the beast?" (Revelation 13:4). The Bible says he will eventually sit in the Temple of God in Jerusalem, claiming to be God, and the people will gather to worship him. Revelation chapter 13 verse 8 says so, and 2 Thessalonians chapter 2 verse 4 says he "exalteth himself above all that is called God, or that is worshipped; so that he as God sitteth in the temple of God, shewing himself that he is God". The people around the world also will worship him. The people will be pleased with him, for besides giving them at last a god they can see and a world religion, he will be a genius—a brilliant scientist, and apparently a man of peace. He will solve the Arab-Israeli problem with a splendid peace treaty which he, himself, will break when it suits him. His physical appearance will be unusual. Arthur E. Bloomfield, speaking of this, says: "Eyes speak of unusual intelligence or knowledge. In this case there is something supernatural about them. Satan's cunning shines through them. Daniel 8:23 says 'And in the latter time of their kingdom, when the transgressors are come to the full, a king of fierce countenance, and understanding dark sentences, shall stand up'. It is probably this feature that captivates the world. It will be almost impossible to resist those eyes. When the world is in a state of hopelessness and terror with no way out, here is a man who seems to know exactly what to do and how to do it. Of course it will be wrong, but it will seem right at the time. Even church leaders will get enthusiastic over him. Everybody will be deceived—except those who recognize him for what he is."

C. THE POWER

Daniel chapter 8 verse 24 says "His power shall be mighty, but not by his own power". His power will come from Satan, but it will not last. Verse 25 of the same chapter says "He shall also stand up against the Prince of princes; but he shall be broken without hand". 2 Thessalonians chapter 2 verse 8 says the Lord shall destroy him "with the brightness of His coming"—when He comes back in power and glory to reign.

His power, as supreme world ruler, will only last three and a half years, but his rise to power will be during the previous three and a half years. His power will be so

great that all people will be required to receive his mark—
"the mark of the Beast"—and without this mark there
will be no buying or selling. There will be death for all
who refuse it. Revelation chapter 13 verses 15 to 18
makes this plain. Today the world is being conditioned
for this. Most people already have a Social Security or
National Insurance number. Without this, as a rule,
there is no work, and certainly there is no Sick Benefit or
Old Age Pension. Then, too, the demands of trade unions
have made it that there is often no job unless one has a
union card or number. People today are being prepared
to accept the Beast and his mark. Dr. John Wesley
White in his book *Re-entry* tells us: "There is now a process
whereby a number can be imprinted invisibly and irre-
movably on your hand or forehead by an electronic device
and with an instrument can be read at a glance.
Increasingly, numbers are replacing names in our world."

The apostle Paul says in 2 Thessalonians chapter 2
verse 9 that the Beast with his great power will be "after
the working of Satan with all power and signs and lying
wonders". The world will be deceived. The Bible says
in verse 12 of the same chapter that all who reject the
Gospel now—in the Day of Grace—will "be damned"—
that is, lost eternally. Today, all may repent of their sin
and put their trust in the Lord Jesus Christ as Saviour.
He is coming soon!

D. THE PROGRAM

The Beast, along with his colleague the False Prophet,
will deceive the world. They will establish a form of
world government. They will create a world religion.
They will appear to succeed even although during the last
three and a half years of the Tribulation Period God's
judgments will be poured out on the earth. But—they
are doomed! The Bible says that they will end in the
Lake of Fire. Revelation chapter 19 describes the return
of the Lord in power and glory. At that point in history
the Beast will be leading the world's armies at the battle

of Armageddon in Israel.   The Lord then descends from
heaven leading His armies, and in verses 19 and 20 we
read: "I saw the beast, and the kings of the earth, and
their armies, gathered together to make war against Him
that sat on the horse, and against His army.   And the
beast was taken, and with him the false prophet that
wrought miracles before him, with which he deceived them
that had received the mark of the beast, and them that
worshipped his image.   These both were cast alive into a
lake of fire burning with brimstone."

Before this, the Beast will have destroyed the World
Church—headed by Romanism and the Ecumenical
Movement.   Then, he will break his treaty with Israel,
and the Jews again will suffer terribly.   Mr. MacPherson
says of this: "Thus will begin in dead earnest what the
Bible calls 'the time of Jacob's trouble' (Jeremiah 30:7),
the most frightful period of Israel's history.   Of it our
Lord Himself declared, 'Then shall be great tribulation,
such as was not since the beginning of the world to this
time, no, nor ever shall be.   And except these days
should be shortened, there should no flesh be saved: but
for the elect's sake (that is, for the sake of the Jewish
remnant) those days shall be shortened' (Matthew 24:21,
22).   This is the vortex and storm-centre of the Great
Tribulation, the hottest area of the colossal conflict.   Not
all the pogroms of Russia, nor all the concentration camps
of Germany have inflicted upon the defenceless Jews one
hundredth part of the horrors of this their darkest hour."

The coming of the King of kings will put an end to the
trouble, and at last there will be peace.   The program of
the Beast is organized!   It will take place soon!   Dr.
DeHaan, however, reminds us that: "There is One Who
now hinders and withholds the revelation of the Man of
Sin.   That One is the Spirit of God, and at the Rapture,
when He is taken out of the way and with the Church,
upon whom He came at Pentecost, rises to meet the Lord
in the air—then and then only will the Antichrist be free
to put his age-old schemes of the devil into operation.

The spirit of the Antichrist is held in check now, while the Spirit is gathering out the bride.   The moment the bride is complete and Christ has gathered out of the Gentiles a people for His Name, then the hindrance will be removed, the personal Antichrist will be revealed and the Day of the Lord will be ushered in."

The Beast Sign is here with us today!   The world wants this man!   He is probably alive today—awaiting the signal to step forward.   This surely is a reminder that Jesus is coming soon!

"Woes are coming—tragic, awesome,
When the Church from earth has gone;
When the One Who now restraineth
No more holds hell's flood-gates down.
When from out the 'sea' of nations
The arch-monster shall appear—
Oh, rejoice ye ransomed pilgrims
That ye will not then be here.

Watch the signs—they quick are showing;
All things say the end is near;
Even now, without our knowing,
Antichrist may now be here.
For earth's week of crushing travail
Quick the stage is being set,
When, unleashed, hell's awesome forces
Make their greatest onslaught yet.

But, beloved, be not shaken,
Christ the Conqueror first must come;
They who are His blood-bought children
He must safely have at Home:
Part they are—oh wondrous prospect—
Of His spotless, holy Bride;
Ere shall burst earth's week of travail
She must be at His blest side."

J. Danson Smith.

CHAPTER 10

THE SPACE SIGN

In Matthew chapter 16 verse 3 the Lord Jesus Christ said to the religious leaders of His day: "Can ye not discern the signs of the times?" This same question can be asked today, but this time in a more exciting situation. In recent times, man has learned the techniques of space travel. He is no longer bounded by planet earth. Astronauts have circled the moon and actually walked upon it. Men can stay in orbit now for months on end. "Can ye not discern the signs of the times?" We are obviously living in the last days before Christ comes back to take control of earth's affairs, and before that happens He will come for His Own blood-washed, redeemed people. Yes, we believe that Space travel is a sure sign of the Saviour's return!

Hal Lindsey, in *The Late Great Planet Earth*, links the subject of space travel with the coming again of the Lord Jesus: "The world caught its breath. Science fiction had prepared man for the incredible feats of the astronauts, but when the reality of the moon landing really hit, it was awesome. . . . Astounding as man's trip to the moon is, there is another trip which many men, women, and children will take some day which will leave the rest of the world gasping. Those who remain on earth at that time will use every invention of the human mind to explain the sudden disappearance of millions of people. Reporters who wrote the historic story of Apollo 11 told how the astronauts collected rocks which may reveal the oldest secrets of the solar system. Those who are alive to tell the story of 'Project Disappearance' will try in vain to describe the happening which will verify the oldest secrets of God's words. . . . It will happen! Some day, a day that only God knows, Jesus Christ is coming to take away all those who believe in Him. He is coming to meet all true believers in the air. Without benefit of science, space suits, or interplanetary rockets, there will be those who will be transported into a glorious place more beautiful, more awesome, than we can possibly comprehend. Earth and all its thrills, excitement, and pleasures will be nothing in contrast to this great event."

The development of interest in Space has largely come about since the conclusion of World War Two. This war, with its Flying Bombs, Rockets, and finally the Atom Bomb, was beginning to show what could be done in earth's atmosphere. Man has probed farther and farther, until today various countries have their Space programs. Rev. Ian MacPherson says: "Take the sign of the manned space-capsule. A. S. Wood has significantly pointed out that the Russians succeeded in putting a man into outer space at Ascensiontide. It would seem that, as the date of the Rapture draws near, humanity is becoming, for the first time in its history, exceedingly space-conscious. Ours is an 'air-minded generation'.... The manned space-capsule is a sign of the times. It will not need nuclear power to elevate the saints. They will rise by a heavenly gravitation to meet their returning Lord."

Space scientists have many ideas and plans which eventually they propose to put into operation. At present, however, with the ever-present possibility of war between the West and the East, it is important to have space scientists concentrating on Spy Satellites and Space Craft which can observe and report back on the situation in unfriendly countries. Recently, the "Jewish Chronicle" reported that the United States Space Centre has a team of experts working on a project to place giant aluminium mirrors on the moon. These would be used for lighting at night, and vast savings of electricity and power would be effected. Other great developments are taking place. Dr. John Wesley White, writing on scientific developments, said: "One of the most fascinating advances in technology, highlighted in the Apollo moon landings, is the planting of the laser beam reflector on the moon surface to get an exact measurement of its distance from the earth. . . . The laser beam of light is revolutionizing many areas of science. It concentrates tremendous energy into a pinpoint of light and generates intense heat. Metals can be welded by it, machine guns and rockets fired by it. In medicine, laser beams are sent through glass fibres to treat growths in inaccessible parts of the body, and detached retinas are rejoined to the eye by their use. In space communication, laser beams are being used to bring television pictures from outer space in seconds, and in industry they have vapourised coal into gas, making hitherto uneconomical coal seams workable.''

Man now is talking seriously of the possibility of building large platforms in space with regular transport between earth and the "space village". Things are advancing so rapidly today that Christ must come soon. Man will not be allowed by God to go too far in his explorations and inventions. Space, however, is the realm of the future and whatever happens there, that is not a top secret item, is generally reported with great excitement. Dr. White goes on to say: "Man has always longed to fly and eventually to ascend into space. In this last third of the twentieth century, man is not only flying billions of man-miles per year, he is ascending, not fictionally, but factually to the skies—into skylabs, on to the moon, and soon, he speculates, to Mars. . . . In the space program, scientists have learned how to hurl man in his craft aloft from the earth and into orbit, at a speed of 19,000 miles per hour, sending him into outer space a quarter of a million miles straight away from the world to the moon. In the airlift of the ages, all the saints of all generations and nations will rise to meet Christ and with Him ascend into heaven. What an event!''

Much more could be written concerning things that are happening in outer space today. Sunspots, increased magnetic activity on the sun, Unidentified Flying Objects and many other things all point to the fact that we live in the last days of the Age of Grace. The time is short for sinners to repent and receive the Saviour! The time is short for the Christian to work!

"Today perhaps!   Perhaps today!
Yes, He may come!   Then watch and pray!
This 'Blessed Hope' keep much in view;
Nor deem it dead tho' taught by few.
And be as urgent as you may
In winning souls while 'tis 'Today'."

J. Danson Smith.

CHAPTER 11

THE TECHNOLOGICAL SIGN

Technology, as shown in the last chapter, has been making very rapid strides forward. The Twentieth Century has seen the most fantastic developments take place. From the slow, jogging pace of life in the previous centuries man has invented and developed a vast number of wonderful things. The prophet Daniel long ago said "Knowledge shall be increased" (Daniel 12:4). This was a very definite reference to the "end times", and we are seeing the increase of knowledge today.

Dr. Walvoord and his son mention some of the recent developments: "By every standard of measurement, the twentieth century will go down in history as the incredible century. The century began with limited use of electricity, without radio, television, planes, missiles, electronic computers, modern weapons, and atomic bombs. Technology has moved man into a modern era which now witnesses more rapid change in the course of a year than formerly took place in a century. The phenomenal scientific developments of our age have exploded in parallel cultural changes. Gigantic manufacturing complexes have arisen; millions of people have moved from rural areas to the city; modern travel has shrunk the world so that everyone is everyone else's neighbour; luxuries, comforts, and pleasures, unknown in previous generations, have become commonplace."

We live in a constantly changing society, and the speed of change is almost frightening. Automatic machinery and computers now do tasks which formerly required many people to handle. As a result people have much more leisure time. Some use it to advantage, while others waste it. Then, again, machines sometimes make workers redundant. In farming, in construction, in mining, and in much of industry technology has made great advances.

Again to repeat the words of Daniel in chapter 12 verse 4 he said: "Knowledge shall be increased". Man may think he is clever but it is God Who has given man this increase in knowledge. He is at the back of the technological advancement. He is speeding things up as this old earth draws towards the end of its period of wickedness before the King of kings takes control.

Dr. M. R. DeHaan, in *Signs of the Times*, says: "Only a few years ago travel was limited. Transportation was mostly by horse and buggy, ox-teams and on foot. When I began practising medicine I made my calls with horse and buggy, or with a cutter in the winter. There was not a mile of paved highway in the entire county. Automobiles were still a novelty. Airplanes were unknown. Few people travelled more than a few miles from their own homes. Then began the travel age, and many began to run to and fro. Today, people travel almost anywhere at will. Trains travel at almost a hundred miles per hour, autos even faster. Fast ships cross the Atlantic in a few days, planes make the trip to Europe in a few hours. The world can be circled in a few days. Our highways are jammed, airplane reservations are sold out, men are running to and fro on every hand. This, says the Word of God, indicates the time of the end. . . . The increase of knowledge in medicine and surgery is indescribable. Such scourges as smallpox, diphtheria, scarlet fever, and typhoid are almost unknown. Today, there is a wealth of knowledge concerning drugs and medicines, antibiotics and vitamins. The progress in surgery, especially heart surgery, and the advance in the conquest of almost every disease is phenomenal. Think how knowledge has increased concerning the structure of matter in the discovery of atomic fission and the greatly increased knowledge of the heavens in astronomy. This advance is true of every field of knowledge."

It is remarkable to read in the Bible the words of James. In his Epistle chapter 5 verses 1 to 3 he says: "Go to now, ye rich men, weep and howl for your miseries that shall come upon you.   Your riches are corrupted, and your garments are motheaten.   Your gold and silver is cankered; and the rust of them shall be a witness against you, and shall eat your flesh as it were fire.   Ye have heaped treasure together for the last days."   Many people think that they must use technology to heap up riches. They find a measure of security in wealth, but they forget that the One Who gave the increase in knowledge also has the power to take away their possessions, and without the Lord Jesus Christ as their personal Saviour they will soon go to a lost eternity.

Again quoting Dr. John Wesley White, he says: "The West and the Middle East are especially rich today because of technology.   Colonel Frank Borman asserts, 'I believe now that man can do anything he wants, technically'. This attitude led Prince Philip to refer to today's 'high priests of science' in an address in which he called universal man to put his faith again in the God Who has provided us with all these good things.   Otherwise, he said, they will turn and devour us."

It is quite apparent to the thinking person that all these recent developments and discoveries are not "by chance". They are indeed God-given—although one has to acknowledge the fact that the nations today are putting much emphasis on learning and education. Rev. Ian MacPherson mentions that: "Not long ago a radio commentator declared that in our day there has been what she called 'a knowledge explosion', and that ninety per cent of all discoveries and inventions date from the beginning of this century, the remaining ten per cent covering all the rest of human history. . . .   Man's achievements in the fields of science and technology have been positively breath-taking. The race has leapt from the penny-farthing to the space-module in a single human lifetime."

In the remaining time before the Lord Jesus comes back

for His Own technology will develop even faster. Exciting things are happening, but for the child of God none will compare with that moment when the trumpet sounds and he is "caught up to meet the Lord in the air"! Then, he shall see the One Who loved us and gave Himself for us.

"We look for the Saviour, we look for His coming,
When living and sleeping shall meet in the skies;
When from every nation, with great jubilation,
The blood-bought unite at the wondrous assize."

J. Danson Smith.

CHAPTER 12

THE MILLENNIAL SIGN

Men have spoken for centuries of the Golden Age that is to come. By their labours and inventions, as well as by God-given increase of knowledge, men have greatly reduced their "working week", and also by the use of machinery they have lessened the need for heavy manual labour. However, these things, along with large increases in money and goods, have not brought to pass the Golden Age! Man is still sinful and wicked, and crime is much on the increase. Is the Golden Age, therefore, a hopeless dream?

The Word of God, which is our only authority, clearly and emphatically speaks of Earth's Golden Age. It is to last for one thousand years, and it will be under the kingship of the Lord Jesus Christ. This kingdom age is mentioned in Revelation chapter 20 verses 4 to 6. It is known as the Millennium.

Today, leaders of the Jewish nation, which is back in the land of Israel after being scattered for almost two thousand years, are looking for the coming of their Messiah or King. Christ is their King, and He is coming soon!

Many great passages in the Bible speak of the Millennium. Take, for example, Isaiah chapter 2 verses 1 to 4, also Psalm 72. Then, Zechariah, in his prophecy in chapter 14 verse 9, says "The Lord shall be King over all the earth". He also describes how the nations will have to attend at Jerusalem each year and "worship the King, the Lord of hosts", and he states that if they fail to do this their land will have no rain (Zechariah 14:16, 17).

Man today longs for peace, but there will not be and can not be real peace until the Prince of Peace comes to reign.

The Millennium will never come by negotiated peace treaties. It will never come through the work of church leaders. It cannot come until the Lord Jesus Christ returns in power and glory to the earth.

Satan and his demons will be bound for a thousand years. Their influence will not be felt. There will be a perfect political government under Christ. The world's economy will be perfect. Truth and righteousness will prevail.

Professor J. Dwight Pentecost, in his tremendous work *Things to Come*, states: "A larger body of prophetic Scripture is devoted to the subject of the millennium, developing its character and conditions, than any other one subject. This millennial age, in which the purposes of God are fully realised on the earth, demands considerable attention. . . . It is evident that there can and will be no earthly theocratic kingdom apart from the personal manifested presence of the Lord Jesus Christ. This whole age depends upon His return to the earth as promised. All that exists in the millennium has its origin in the King Who is revealed. . . . The millennium will be the period of the full manifestation of the glory of the Lord Jesus Christ. There will be the manifestation of glory associated with the humanity of Christ. There will be the glory of a glorious dominion, in which Christ, by virtue of His obedience unto death, is given universal dominion to replace that dominion which Adam lost. There will be the glory of a glorious government, in which Christ, as David's son, is given absolute power to govern (Isaiah 9:6; Psalm 45:4; Isaiah 11:4; Psalm 72:4; Psalm 2:9). There will be the glory of a glorious inheritance, in which the land and the seed promised to Abraham are realized through Christ (Genesis 17:8; 15:7; Daniel 11:16; Daniel 11:41; Daniel 8:9). There will be the glory of a glorious judiciary, in which Christ, as the spokesman for God, announces God's will and law throughout the age (Deuteronomy 18:18, 19; Isaiah 33:21, 22; Acts 3:22; Isaiah 2:3, 4; 42:4). There will be the glory of a glorious house and throne, in which

Christ, as David's son, shall fulfil that promised to David (2 Samuel 7:12-16) in His reign (Isaiah 9:6, 7; Luke 1:31-33; Matthew 25:21).   There will be the glory of a glorious kingdom over which Christ reigns (Psalm 72; Isaiah 11:10; Jeremiah 23:6; Zechariah 3:10; Isaiah 9:7)."

Before all this the Great Tribulation will take place. The Man of Sin—the Antichrist—will have his period of world domination.   The judgments of God will descend upon a Christ-rejecting world.   Prior to all these things the Saviour will have come to the air and taken His Own out from the world.   This coming will be secret.   His return as King will be glorious and triumphant.   Matthew 24 verse 27 says: "For as the lightning cometh out of the east, and shineth even unto the west; so shall also the coming of the Son of man be".   Revelation chapter 1 verse 7 says "Behold, He cometh with clouds; and every eye shall see Him".   Matthew chapter 24 verse 30 says the whole world "shall see the Son of man coming in the clouds of heaven with power and great glory".

Dr. Oswald J. Smith describes the Lord's return to the earth in this manner: "As He went, He returns.   Amid the clouds of heaven He descends.   Openly He left, openly He comes back.   And all the power is His, while the glory no tongue can describe. . . .   Surely the hour is at hand. The Great Tribulation must be almost upon us, the fearful reign of the Antichrist about to commence.   And then the battle of Armageddon, and then—the glorious revelation of our blessed Lord.   And then, ah, then, at last, the Golden Age, the Millennium.   Hasten, glad day! Hasten, judgment and tribulation!   Hasten, oh hasten, Thou Christ of God, Thou mighty Prince of Peace!"

A. The King and the Kingdom

It is interesting to note in studying the Bible how Matthew reveals the Lord Jesus Christ as "King".   His Gospel frequently refers to the King and the kingdom. The world knows that Israel's King was rejected.   Today, although they know Him not, He is expected! He will be their King. Also, He will be the world's King!

Dr. Lehman Strauss helpfully explains that: "Some err greatly in confusing the kingdom with the Church. Well-meaning Christians often fail to distinguish between the two. I have been in churches where pastors, or church officers, have prayed for the advancement of the kingdom. God's purpose for this age is the building of His Church. The kingdom cannot be established until the King returns, and this He will not do until He has finished building His Church. . . . The Church Age will end at the Rapture, when Jesus comes in the air to catch away the redeemed; the Kingdom Age will not commence until the King returns the second time with His Own redeemed ones and all the holy angels with Him."

The day is approaching fast when Christ's kingdom will be here. Nearly three hundred years ago Isaac Watts reminded us that:

> "Jesus shall reign where'er the sun
> Doth his successive journeys run;
> His kingdom stretch from shore to shore,
> Till moons shall wax and wane no more."

His kingdom will be world-wide. Everyone will come under its control. The Bible says that Christ will "rule with a rod of iron" (Revelation 19:15). In Philippians chapter 2 verses 10 and 11 we read "that at the name of Jesus every knee should bow . . . and that every tongue should confess that Jesus Christ is Lord, to the glory of God the Father".

B. THE KINGDOM'S INFLUENCE

The Millennium will see vast changes on earth. Animal life, for instance, will return to Edenic conditions. It was because of man's sin that the animal realm suffered. Isaiah chapter 11 describes the coming Kingdom and in verses 6 to 8 we read: "The wolf also shall dwell with the lamb, and the leopard shall lie down with the kid; and the calf and the young lion and the fatling together; and a little child shall lead them. And the cow and the bear shall feed; their young ones shall lie down together: and the lion shall eat straw like the ox. And the sucking child shall play on the hole of the asp, and the weaned child shall put his hand on the cockatrice' den."

Dr. John R. Rice describes the Kingdom's influence in these words: "What a great change in animal nature! The wolf, leopard and young lion will no longer be beasts of prey and will do no harm to the lamb, the kid and the fat calf. A child can play, in that day, with the beasts of the field, as might today with a puppy. There will be no more carnivorous beasts, but 'the lion shall eat straw like the ox'! . . . We may be sure that that change will reach even to insects and disease germs. If the lion will eat straw like the ox, and wolves, leopards, and poisonous snakes will be safe playmates for the babies, we may be sure that people in that happy time will be safe from the sting of insects, from infection and bacteria or from harm by any of God's creatures."

Then, also, the Millennium will see the curse on the ground lifted. Weeds, thorns and thistles will cease to grow. Isaiah chapter 35, speaking of the Millennium, says "the desert shall rejoice, and blossom as the rose". Amos chapter 9 verse 13, speaking of the influence of the Kingdom, says that "the plowman shall overtake the reaper". Crops will be most abundant. Human life, too, will be greatly prolonged in the Millennial Age, and life will be vastly different under the rule of the King. Dr. John Wesley White indicates some of the changes that are coming: "Under His universal reign, humanity will rise to heights of happiness never before realised, or even dreamed of, in the history of man on this planet. It is my belief that with science and technology yielding such unprecedented progress today, unhampered by crime, war and hate, as they will be under the benevolent reign of Jesus, every invention will be utilised for man's freedom and fulfilment here on the earth—for a thousand years."

C. THE BRIDE OF THE KING

The True Church is the Bride of Christ. Every boy and girl, every man and woman down through the ages who has acknowledged himself to be a sinner and has asked the Lord Jesus Christ to save them is a member of the True Church. As we have seen already, Christ is coming for His Bride soon—at any moment! She will be caught up to meet Him in the air, (I Thessalonians 4:16, 17). Then, after certain events—the Marriage Supper of the Lamb, and the Judgment Seat of Christ—the Church along with her heavenly Bridegroom returns to earth to reign with Him.

As Dr. Pentecost says: "When Jesus Christ comes to this earth to reign, He is not going to leave His beloved Bride behind. He is not going to separate Himself from the Church of which He is the living Head. He is going to bring this body of redeemed ones with Him, so that He might be glorified in the saints and that they might share His glory. As the bride of a king shares in the glory, the privileges, the honours of her husband's throne, so we through the age of the King's reign will share His glory, and His honour. Thus will be fulfilled His promise, 'And if I go and prepare a place for you, I will come again, and receive you unto Myself; that where I am, there ye may be also' (John 14:3). As He reigns as King of kings and Lord of lords for ever and ever, we shall share His glory."

The Millennial reign of Christ is near. Soon, He will be seen by the world's population leading the armies of heaven—descending to the Mount of Olives from whence He went at His ascension. Jerusalem will become a sea-port and the centre of the world's attention. Today, that city and the land of Israel are focal points in most news bulletins. The Millennial sign is here! The King is coming!

"Oh, the glory of that coming,
When He comes as King of kings;
When ten thousand times ten thousand
Ransomed souls with Him He brings;

When, with them, we stand before Him,
Clothed, but in immortal dress,
Finite mind must fail to picture
Such exceeding gloriousness."

J. Danson Smith.

CHAPTER 13

A SOLEMN WARNING

In the foregoing chapters we have considered rather briefly some of the Signs of the Saviour's Return. Without any doubt we live in momentous times. Down through the ages, some of the signs of Christ's return were apparent, but today ALL the signs are present together! The Saviour Himself gave this solemn warning in Matthew chapter 24 verse 44 "Therefore be ye also ready for in such an hour as ye think not the Son of man cometh".

The true child of God who reads His Word and believes it in its entirety is waiting and looking for the Saviour to come at any moment. His life, therefore, should be lived in the light of the Saviour's return. This will affect his thinking, his working, his witnessing and his planning.

Dr. John R. Rice makes this challenge: "Those who know they are saved should so live that they will not be ashamed before Christ at His coming. This duty of all Christians to be ready for Jesus is expressed in 1 John 2:28 which says: 'And now, little children, abide in Him; that, when He shall appear, we may have confidence, and not be ashamed before Him at His coming'. I know I am saved, and therefore when Jesus comes, I will go with Him. But a child of God who is not on duty, not winning souls, not living right will be ashamed before Christ when He comes. We will go with Christ to the wedding supper, but we should also remember that we go to the judgment seat of Christ. We must give an account of our stewardship and receive our reward."

Many today who are members of churches—religious, baptized people—are not "ready". There is but one way to be "ready", and that is by asking the Saviour into one's own heart. "He is able to save"—so the Bible says! He is waiting to save YOU as you read this—if only you will acknowledge the fact that you are a sinner. His precious blood was shed on Calvary to make atonement for sin. Because Adam sinned every human being is born a sinner. However, the Lord Jesus Christ is the last Adam, and His death and the precious blood which He shed deliberately on the Cross will clear your sin, if you ask Him to save you now. He has said in His Word: "Him that cometh to Me I will in no wise cast out" (John 6:37). The apostle Paul says in 1 Corinthians chapter 15 verse 22: "As in Adam all die, even so in Christ shall all be made alive". The apostle John in his 1st Epistle chapter 5 verses 11 and 12 says: "This is the record, that God hath given to us eternal life, and this life is in His Son. He that hath the Son hath life; and he that hath not the Son of God hath not life." We either have, or we have not! "Be ye also ready."

Years ago, W. E. Blackstone said in his book *Jesus is Coming*: "Dear friend, we point you to the crucified Saviour as the only hope of salvation. We beg of you to 'kiss the Son, lest ye perish from the way. . . . Blessed are all they that put their trust in Him' (Psalm 2:12). What shall it profit you if you gain the whole world and lose your own soul? (Matthew 16:26, 27). He is coming, and we know neither the day, nor the hour when He may come, (Matthew 25:13). What if He should come now? Would you be found of Him in peace (2 Peter 3:14), or would you be left behind to endure the terrible things which shall come upon the world (Luke 21:25, 26), while the Church is with Christ in the air (Luke 21:36 and 1 Thessalonians 4:17), and be made at His appearing (2 Thessalonians 1:7-10) to mourn (Matthew 24:30) and pray to the mountains and rocks to hide you from His face (Revelation 6:16)? 'Prepare to meet thy God' was the solemn injunction to Israel (Amos 4:12), and every one of us, both Jew and Gentile, must meet Him either in grace or in judgment."

The signs of the Saviour's return as King of kings and Lord of lords abound. The Lord Jesus Christ said in Luke chapter 21 verse 28: "When these things begin to come to pass, then look up . . . for your redemption draweth nigh". No one can deny this. For the true Christian this is a "blessed hope". For those not saved, His coming to the air will herald in the Great Tribulation and afterwards a lost eternity in hell.

Dr. John R. Rice, the great evangelist, warns: "If you are left here when the Christian people are taken away, you are likely to commit the unpardonable sin. Multitudes will, for every one whose name is not written in the book of life will take the mark of the beast, the Man of Sin; and when one does, he will be forever lost, with no chance to escape. When mother and sister and wife are taken away, when every true church is closed, and when every saved person is gone, what will you do? The most likely thing is that you will lose your soul. It is wicked to delay. The Scriptures say: 'Today if ye will hear His voice, harden not your hearts'. Now is God's time. You can be saved right now if you will in your heart put your trust in Jesus."

I wish to close with the words of my father—J. Danson Smith—as he gives you, dear reader, a final invitation to "be ready", and you can respond—even now!

"God has not promised to save you tomorrow,
　But He has promised to hear you today;
　Why risk salvation when you cannot borrow
　One single moment, much less a new day?

　God has not promised to save you tomorrow,
　But He is waiting to save you today;
　Why should you linger in sadness and sorrow,
　Why do you tarry, oh, why still delay?

　Yes, God has promised eternal redemption
　For every soul who will trust Him today;
　Freedom from guilt, and from sin full exemption,
　But His great promise is just for today.

Only today is the day of salvation,
Only today is God's offer to you;
Only today is the great invitation,
Will you take Christ—today?"

BIBLIOGRAPHY

Beckwith, George D., *God's Prophetic Plan*
   Grand Rapids: Zondervan Publishing House, 1962.
Blackstone, W. E., *Jesus is Coming*
   Glasgow: Pickering and Inglis Ltd.
   U.S.A.: Fleming H. Revell Co., 1898.
Bloomfield, Arthur E., *Before the Last Battle—Armageddon*
   Minneapolis: Bethany Fellowship Inc., 1971.
DeHaan, Dr. M. R., *Signs of the Times*
   Grand Rapids: Zondervan Publishing House, 1951.
DeHaan, Dr. M. R., *The Second Coming of Jesus*
   Grand Rapids: Zondervan Publishing House, 1944.
DeHaan, Richard, *Israel and the Nations in Prophecy*
   Grand Rapids: Zondervan Publishing House, 1977.
Douglas, Rev. John, *The Charismatic Movement*
   Belfast: Puritan Printing Co., 1978.
Duty, Guy, *Christ's Coming and the World Church*
   Minneapolis: Bethany Fellowship Inc., 1971.
Duty, Guy, *Escape from the Coming Tribulation*
   Minneapolis: Bethany Fellowship Inc., 1975.
Feinberg, Charles Lee, *Prophecy and the Seventies*
   Chicago: Moody Bible Institute, 1971.
Hamilton, Gavin, *The Rapture and the Great Tribulation*
   Oak Park: The Author, 1957.
Kirban, Salem, *Guide to Survival*
   Wheaton: Tyndale House Publishers, 1968.
Langston, Rev. E. L., *How God is Working to a Plan*
   London: Marshall, Morgan and Scott Ltd., about 1940.
Lindsey, Hal, *The Late Great Planet Earth*
   Grand Rapids: Zondervan Publishing House, 1970.
Lindsey, Hal, *Satan is Alive and Well on Planet Earth*
   Grand Rapids: Zondervan Publishing House, 1972.
Logsdon, Dr. S. Franklin, *Profiles of Prophecy*
   Grand Rapids: Zondervan Publishing House, 1970.
MacPherson, Rev. Ian, *News of the World to Come*
   Eastbourne: Prophetic Witness Publishing House, 1975.

Malgo, Wim, *Shadows of Armageddon*
          Hamilton: Midnight Call Inc., 1976.
Paisley, Rev. Ian R. K., D.D., M.P., *The World Council of Churches*
          Belfast: The Author, about 1965.
Pentecost, Professor J. Dwight, Th.D., *Prophecy for Today*
          Grand Rapids: Zondervan Publishing House, 1961.
Pentecost, Professor J. Dwight, Th.D., *Things to Come*
          Findlay: Dunham Publishing Co., 1958.
Rice, John R., D.D., Litt.D., *The Coming Kingdom of Christ*
          Murfreesboro: Sword of the Lord Publishers, 1945.
Ritchie, John, *Impending Great Events*
          Glasgow: Pickering and Inglis Ltd., 1938.
Smith, J. and T. C. Danson, *Coming Soon*
          Edinburgh: B. McCall Barbour, 1978.
Smith, Oswald J., Litt.D., *Prophecy—What Lies Ahead?*
          London: Marshall, Morgan and Scott Ltd., about 1942.
Strauss, Lehman, Litt.D., *The End of This Present World*
          Grand Rapids: Zondervan Publishing House, 1967.
Tenney, Merrill C., Ph.D., *Zondervan Pictorial Bible Dictionary*
          Grand Rapids: Zondervan Publishing House, 1963.
Trumbull, Charles G., Litt.D., *Prophecy's Light on Today*
          London: Oliphants Ltd., about 1938.
Walvoord, John F., Th.D., *The Church in Prophecy*
          Grand Rapids: Zondervan Publishing House, 1964.
Walvoord, John F., Th.D., *The Return of the Lord*
          Findlay: Dunham Publishing Co., 1955.
Walvoord, John F. and John E., *Armageddon Oil and the Middle East Crisis*
          Grand Rapids: Zondervan Publishing House, 1974.
White, John Wesley, Ph.D., *Re-entry*
          Grand Rapids: Zondervan Publishing House, 1970.
White, John Wesley, Ph.D., *W.W. III*
          Grand Rapids: Zondervan Publishing House, 1977.

Another challenging and enlightening book
by T. C. DANSON SMITH
'FROM THE RAINBOW TO THE RAPTURE'

A great study book, covering Genesis to Revelation. In it the author shows how God has a plan, and in every age He has offered man the two alternatives—Judgment for sin or Salvation through the blood. This book is a challenge to the Christian, and it also presents the Gospel clearly to all who are not saved.

'The book makes an ideal gift for Christian or non-Christian.'
New Life

'This book is to be welcomed, for it develops a theme that has been helpful to many, namely the dispensational dealings of God. . . . The author believes in the impeccability of Christ, the value of the blood, the pre-millennial rapture of the believers of the Church age and the literal one thousand years reign of Christ. The orthodox approach commends it to a wide audience; its simple style makes it suitable even for younger readers. . . . We trust many will buy this book.'   *Believers Magazine*

'A very interesting, clear and helpful study.'
A Bookstall's Newsletter

Other commendations include:

'This is what our younger people need today—most challenging and helpful.'   .   *From a leading preacher*

'This book is a treasure.'   *From Australia*

'The contents are sound, refreshing and edifying to the believer and incisive in its warning to the unconverted of the simple and solemn choice laid before them.'
From a well-known evangelist

Published by
B. McCALL BARBOUR
28 George IV Bridge, Edinburgh EH1 1ES, Scotland